The Account of Mary Rowlandson
and Other
Indian Captivity Narratives

The Account of Mary Rowlandson
and Other
Indian Captivity Narratives

Mary Rowlandson
and Others

Edited by
Horace Kephart

DOVER PUBLICATIONS, INC.
Mineola, New York

Bibliographical Note

This Dover edition, first published in 2005, is an unabridged republication of *Captives Among the Indians,* published by Outing Publishing Company, New York, 1915.

Library of Congress Cataloging-in-Publication Data

Captives among the Indians.
    The account of Mary Rowlandson and other Indian captivity narratives / Mary Rowlandson and others ; edited by Horace Kephart.
        p. cm.
    Originally published: Captives among the Indians. New York : Outing Pub. Co., 1915, in series: Outing adventure library; no. 3.
    ISBN-13: 978-0-486-44520-5 (pbk.)
    ISBN-10: 0-486-44520-8 (pbk.)
    1. Indian captivities—Northeastern States. I. Rowlandson, Mary White, ca. 1635–1711. II. Kephart, Horace, 1862–1931. III. Title.

E85.K38 2005
973.2'092'2—dc22

                                                          2005045460

Manufactured in the United States by Courier Corporation
44520806   2013
www.doverpublications.com

Contents

Col. James Smith's Life Among the Delawares, 1755–1759

JAMES SMITH, pioneer, was born in Franklin county, Pennsylvania, in 1737. When he was eighteen years of age he was captured by the Indians, was adopted into one of their tribes, and lived with them as one of themselves until his escape in 1759.

He became a lieutenant under General Bouquet during the expedition against the Ohio Indians in 1764, and was captain of a company of rangers in Lord Dunmore's War. In 1775 he was promoted to major of militia. He served in the Pennsylvania convention in 1776, and in the assembly in 1776–77. In the latter year he was commissioned colonel in command on the frontiers, and performed distinguished services.

Smith moved to Kentucky in 1788. He was a member of the Danville convention, and represented Bourbon county for many years in the legislature. He died in Washington county, Kentucky, in 1812.

The following narrative of his experience as member of an Indian tribe is from his own book entitled "Remarkable Adventures in the Life and Travels of Colonel James Smith," printed at Lexington, Kentucky, in 1799. It affords a striking contrast to the terrible experiences of the other captives whose stories are republished in this book; for he was well treated, and stayed so long with his red captors that he acquired expert knowledge of their arts and customs, and deep insight into their character. (*Editor.*)

IN May, 1755, the province of Pennsylvania agreed to send out three hundred men, in order to cut a wagon-road from Fort Loudon, to join Braddock's road, near the Turkey Foot, or three forks of Youghigheny. My brother-in-law, William Smith, Esq., of Conococheague, was appointed commissioner, to have the oversight of these road-cutters.

Though I was at that time only eighteen years of age, I had fallen violently in love with a young lady, whom I apprehended was possessed of a large share of both beauty and virtue; but being born between Venus and Mars, I concluded I must also leave my dear fair one, and go out with this company of road-cutters to see the event of this campaign; but still expecting that some time in the course of this summer I should again return to the arms of my beloved.

We went on with the road, without interruption, until near the Alleghany mountain; when I was sent back in order to hurry up some provision-wagons that were on the way after us. I proceeded down the road as far as the crossings of Juniata, where, finding the wagons were coming on as fast as possible, I returned up the road again towards the Alleghany mountain, in company with one Arnold Vigoras. About four or five miles above Bedford, three Indians had made a blind of bushes, stuck in the ground as though they grew naturally, where they concealed themselves, about fifteen yards from the road. When we came opposite to them they fired upon us, at this short distance, and killed my fellow-traveller, yet their bullets did not touch me; but my horse making a violent start, threw me, and the Indians immediately ran up and took me prisoner. The one who laid hold on me was a Canasatauga, the other two were Delawares. One of them could speak English, and asked me if there were any more white men coming after. I told them not any near that I knew of. Two of these Indians stood by me, while the other scalped my comrade; they then set off and ran at a smart rate through the woods, for about fifteen miles, and that night we slept on the Alleghany mountain without fire.

The next morning they divided the last of their provisions which they had brought from Fort Du Quesne, and gave me an equal share, which was about two or three ounces of mouldy biscuit; this and a young ground-hog, about as large as a rabbit, roasted, and also equally divided, was all the provision we had until we came to the Loyal Hannan, which was about fifty miles; and a great part of the way we came through exceeding rocky laurel-thickets without any path. When we came to the west side of Laurel hill, they gave the scalp halloo, as usual, which is a long yell or halloo for every scalp or prisoner they have in possession; the last of these scalp halloos were followed with quick and sudden shrill shouts of joy and triumph. On their performing this, we were answered by the firing of a number of guns on the Loyal Hannan, one after another, quicker than one could count, by another party of Indians who were encamped near where Ligonier now stands. As we advanced near this party, they increased with repeated shouts of joy and triumph; but I did not share with them in their excessive mirth. When we came to this camp we found they had plenty of turkeys and other meat there; and though I never before ate venison without bread or salt, yet as I was hungry it relished very well. There we lay that night, and the next morning the whole of us marched on our way for Fort Du Quesne. The night after we joined another camp of Indians, with nearly the same ceremony, attended with great noise, and apparent joy, among all except one. The next morning we continued our march, and in the afternoon we came in full view of the fort, which stood on the point, near where Fort Pitt[1] now stands. We then made a halt on the bank of the Alleghany, and repeated the scalp halloo, which was answered by the firing of all the firelocks in the hands of both Indians and French who were in and about the fort, in the aforesaid manner, and also the great guns, which were followed by the continued shouts and yells of the different savage tribes who were then collected there.

As I was at this time unacquainted with this mode of firing and yelling of the savages, I concluded that there were thousands of Indians there ready to receive General Braddock; but what added to my surprise, I saw numbers running towards me, stripped naked, excepting breech-clouts, and painted in the most hideous manner, of various colors, though the principal color was vermilion, or a bright red; yet there was annexed to this black, brown, blue, etc. As they approached, they formed themselves into two long ranks, about two or three rods apart. I was told by an Indian that could speak English that I must run

---

[1] Pittsburgh.

betwixt these ranks, and that they would flog me all the way as I ran; and if I ran quick, it would be so much the better, as they would quit when I got to the end of the ranks. There appeared to be a general rejoicing around me, yet I could find nothing like joy in my breast; but I started to the race with all the resolution and vigor I was capable of exerting, and found that it was as I had been told, for I was flogged the whole way. When I had got near the end of the lines I was struck with something that appeared to me to be a stick, or the handle of a tomahawk, which caused me to fall to the ground. On my recovering my senses I endeavored to renew my race; but, as I arose, some one cast sand in my eyes, which blinded me so that I could not see where to run. They continued beating me most intolerably, until I was at length insensible; but before I lost my senses I remember my wishing them to strike the fatal blow, for I thought they intended killing me, but apprehended they were too long about it.

The first thing I remember was my being in the fort amidst the French and Indians, and a French doctor standing by me, who had opened a vein in my left arm: after which the interpreter asked me how I did. I told him I felt much pain. The doctor then washed my wounds, and the bruised places of my body with French brandy. As I felt faint, and the brandy smelt well, I asked for some inwardly, but the doctor told me, by the interpreter, that it did not suit my case.

When they found I could speak, a number of Indians came around me, and examined me, with threats of cruel death if I did not tell the truth. The first question they asked me was how many men were there in the party that were coming from Pennsylvania to join Braddock? I told them the truth, that there were three hundred. The next question was, were they well armed? I told them they were all well armed (meaning the arm of flesh), for they had only about thirty guns among the whole of them; which if the Indians had known they would certainly have gone and cut them all off; therefore I could not in conscience let them know the defenceless situation of these road-cutters. I was then sent to the hospital, and carefully attended by the doctors, and recovered quicker than what I expected.

Some time after I was there, I was visited by the Delaware

Indian already mentioned, who was at the taking of me, and could speak some English. Though he spoke but bad English, yet I found him to be a man of considerable understanding. I asked him if I had done anything that had offended the Indians which caused them to treat me so unmercifully. He said no; it was only an old custom the Indians had, and it was like "how do you do"; after that, he said, I would be well used. I asked him if I should be admitted to remain with the French. He said no; and told me that as soon as I recovered, I must not only go with the Indians, but must be made an Indian myself. I asked him what news from Braddock's army. He said the Indians spied them every day, and he showed me, by making marks on the ground with a stick, that Braddock's army was advancing in very close order, and that the Indians would surround them, take trees, and (as he expressed it) *shoot um down all one pigeon.*

Shortly after this, on the 9th day of July, 1755, in the morning, I heard a great stir in the fort. As I could then walk with a staff in my hand, I went out of the door, which was just by the wall of the fort, and stood upon the wall, and viewed the Indians in a huddle before the gate, where were barrels of powder, bullets, flints, etc., and every one taking what suited. I saw the Indians also march off in rank entire; likewise the French Canadians, and some regulars. After viewing the Indians and French in different positions, I computed them to be about four hundred, and wondered that they attempted to go out against Braddock with so small a party. I was then in high hopes that I would soon see them fly before the British troops, and that General Braddock would take the fort and rescue me.

I remained anxious to know the event of this day; and, in the afternoon, I again observed a great noise and commotion in the fort, and though at that time I could not understand French, yet I found that it was the voice of joy and triumph, and feared that they had received what I called bad news.

I had observed some of the old-country soldiers speak Dutch: as I spoke Dutch, I went to one of them, and asked him what was the news. He told me that a runner had just arrived, who said that Braddock would certainly be defeated; that the Indians and French had surrounded him, and were concealed behind trees and in gullies, and kept a constant fire upon the English, and that they saw the English falling in heaps, and if they did not take the river, which was the only gap, and make their escape, there would not be one man left alive before sundown. The morning after the battle I saw Braddock's artillery brought into the fort; the same day I also saw several Indians in British officers' dress, with sash, half-moon, laced hats, etc., which the British then wore.

A few days after this the Indians demanded me, and I was obliged to go with them. I was not yet well able to march, but they took me in a canoe up the Alleghany River to an Indian town that was on the north side of the river, about forty miles above Fort Du Quesne. Here I remained about three weeks, and was then taken to an Indian town on the west branch of Muskingum, about twenty miles above the forks, which was called Tullihas, inhabited by Delawares, Caughnewagas, and Mohicans.

The day after my arrival at the aforesaid town a number of Indians collected about me, and one of them began to pull the hair out of my head. He had some ashes on a piece of bark, in which he frequently dipped his fingers in order to take the firmer hold, and so he went on, as if he had been plucking a turkey, until he had all the hair clean out of my head except a small spot about three or four inches square on my crown; this they cut off with a pair of scissors, excepting three locks, which they dressed up in their own mode. Two of these they wrapped round with a narrow beaded garter made by themselves for that purpose, and the other they plaited at full length, and then stuck it full of silver brooches. After this they bored my nose and ears, and fixed me off with earrings and nose jewels; then they ordered me to strip off my clothes and put on a breechclout, which I did; they then painted my head, face, and body in various colors. They put a large belt of wampum on my neck, and silver bands on my hands and right arm; and so an old chief led me out in the street, and gave the alarm halloo, *coowigh*, several times repeated quick; and on this, all that were in the town came running and stood round the old chief, who held me by the hand in the midst. As I at that time knew nothing of their mode of adoption, and had seen them put to death all they had taken, and as I never could find that they saved a man alive at

Braddock's defeat, I made no doubt but they were about putting me to death in some cruel manner. The old chief, holding me by the hand, made a long speech, very loud, and when he had done, he handed me to three young squaws, who led me by the hand down the bank, into the river, until the water was up to our middle. The squaws then made signs to me to plunge myself into the water, but I did not understand them; I thought that the result of the council was that I should be drowned, and that these young ladies were to be the executioners. They all three laid violent hold of me, and I for some time opposed them with all my might, which occasioned loud laughter by the multitude that were on the bank of the river. At length one of the squaws made out to speak a little English (for I believe they began to be afraid of me), and said *no hurt you.* On this I gave myself up to their ladyships, who were as good as their word; for though they plunged me under water, and washed and rubbed me severely, yet I could not say they hurt me much.

These young women then led me up to the council-house, where some of the tribe were ready with new clothes for me. They gave me a new ruffled shirt, which I put on, also a pair of leggings done off with ribbons and beads, likewise a pair of moccasons and garters dressed with beads, porcupine quills, and red hair—also a tinsel-laced cappo. They again painted my head and face with various colors, and tied a bunch of red feathers to one of those locks they had left on the crown of my head, which stood up five or six inches. They seated me on a bearskin, and gave me a pipe, tomahawk, and pole-cat skin pouch, which had been skinned pocket fashion, and contained tobacco, kille-genico, or dry sumach leaves, which they mix with their tobacco; also spunk, flint, and steel. When I was thus seated, the Indians came in dressed and painted in their grandest manner. As they came in they took their seats, and for a considerable time there was a profound silence—every one was smoking; but not a word was spoken among them. At length one of the chiefs made a speech, which was delivered to me by an interpreter, and was as followeth: "My son, you are now flesh of our flesh, and bone of our bone. By the ceremony which was performed this day every drop of white blood was washed out of your veins; you are taken into the Caughnewaga nation, and initiated into a warlike tribe;

you are adopted into a great family, and now received with great seriousness and solemnity in the room and place of a great man. After what has passed this day, you are now one of us by an old strong law and custom. My son, you have now nothing to fear— we are now under the same obligations to love, support, and defend you that we are to love and to defend one another; therefore, you are to consider yourself as one of our people." At this time I did not believe this fine speech, especially that of the white blood being washed out of me; but since that time I have found out that there was much sincerity in said speech; for, from that day, I never knew them to make any distinction between me and themselves in any respect whatever until I left them. If they had plenty of clothing, I had plenty; if we were scarce, we all shared one fate.

After this ceremony was over I was introduced to my new kin, and told that I was to attend a feast that evening, which I did. And as the custom was, they gave me also a bowl and a wooden spoon, which I carried with me to the place where there was a number of large brass kettles full of boiled venison and green corn; every one advanced with his bowl and spoon, and had his share given him. After this, one of the chiefs made a short speech, and then we began to eat.

Shortly after this I went out to hunt in company with Mohawk Solomon, some of the Caughnewagas, and a Delaware Indian that was married to a Caughnewaga squaw. We travelled about south from this town, and the first night we killed nothing, but we had with us green corn, which we roasted and ate that night. The next day we encamped about twelve o'clock, and the hunters turned out to hunt, and I went down the run that we encamped on, in company with some squaws and boys, to hunt plums, which we found in great plenty. On my return to camp I observed a large piece of fat meat; the Delaware Indian, that could talk some English, observed me looking earnestly at this meat, and asked me, "What meat you think that is?" I said I supposed it was bear meat; he laughed, and said, "Ho, all one fool you, beal now elly pool," and pointing to the other side of the camp, he said, "Look at that skin, you think that beal skin?" I went and lifted the skin, which appeared like an ox-hide; he then said, "What skin you think that?" I replied, that I thought it was a buffalo-hide; he laughed, and said, "You fool again, you know nothing, you think buffalo that colo'?" I acknowledged I did not know much about these things, and told him I never saw a buffalo, and that I had not heard what color they were. He replied, "By and by you shall see gleat many buffalo; he now go to gleat lick. That skin no buffalo-skin, that skin buck-elk-skin." They went out with horses, and brought in the remainder of this buck-elk, which was the fattest creature I ever saw of the tallow kind.

We remained at this camp about eight or ten days, and killed a number of deer. Though we had neither bread nor salt at this time, yet we had both roast and boiled meat in great plenty, and they were frequently inviting me to eat when I had no appetite.

We then moved to the buffalo lick, where we killed several buffalo, and in their small brass kettles they made about half a bushel of salt. I suppose this lick was about thirty or forty miles from the aforesaid town, and somewhere between the Muskingum, Ohio, and Sciota. About the lick was clear, open woods, and thin white-oak land, and at that time there were large roads leading to the lick, like wagon-roads. We moved from this lick about six or seven miles, and encamped on a creek.

Some time after this, I was told to take the dogs with me, and go down the creek, perhaps I might kill a turkey; it being in the afternoon, I was also told not to go far from the creek, and to come up the creek again to the camp, and to take care not to get lost. When I had gone some distance down the creek, I came upon fresh buffalo tracks, and as I had a number of dogs with me to stop the buffalo, I concluded I would follow after and kill one; and as the grass and weeds were rank, I could readily follow the track. A little before sundown I despaired of coming up with them. I was then thinking how I might get to camp before night. I concluded, as the buffalo had made several turns, if I took the track back to the creek it would be dark before I could get to camp; therefore I thought I would take a near way through the hills, and strike the creek a little below the camp; but as it was cloudy weather, and I a very young woodsman, I could find neither creek nor camp. When night came on I fired my gun several times, and hallooed, but could have no answer.

The next morning, early, the Indians were out after me, and as I had with me ten or a dozen dogs, and the grass and weeds rank, they could readily follow my track. When they came up with me they appeared to be in very good-humor. I asked Solomon if he thought I was running away; he said, "No, no, you go too much clooked." On my return to camp they took my gun from me, and for this rash step I was reduced to a bow and arrows for near two years. We were out on this tour for about six weeks.

This country is generally hilly, though intermixed with considerable quantities of rich upland and some good bottoms.

When we returned to the town, Pluggy and his party had arrived, and brought with them a considerable number of scalps and prisoners from the south branch of the Potomac; they also brought with them an English Bible, which they gave to a Dutch woman who was a prisoner; but as she could not read English, she made a present of it to me, which was very acceptable.

I remained in this town until some time in October, when my adopted brother, called Tontileaugo, who had married a Wyandot squaw, took me with him to Lake Erie. On this route we had no horses with us, and when we started from the town all the pack I carried was a pouch containing my books, a little dried venison, and my blanket. I had then no gun, but Tontileaugo, who was a first-rate hunter, carried a rifle gun, and every day killed deer, raccoons, or bears. We left the meat, excepting a little for present use, and carried the skins with us until we encamped, and then stretched them with elm bark, in a frame made with poles stuck in the ground, and tied together with lynn or elm bark; and when the skins were dried by the fire, we packed them up and carried them with us the next day.

As Tontileaugo could not speak English, I had to make use of all the Caughnewaga I had learned, even to talk very imperfectly with him; but I found I learned to talk Indian faster this way than when I had those with me who could speak English.

As we proceeded down the Canesadooharie waters, our packs increased by the skins that were daily killed, and became so very heavy that we could not march more than eight or ten miles per day. We came to Lake Erie about six miles west of the mouth of Canesadooharie. As the wind was very high the evening we came to the lake, I was surprised to hear the roaring of the water, and see the high waves that dashed against the shore, like the ocean. We encamped on a run near the lake, and, as the wind fell that night, the next morning the lake was only in a moderate motion, and we marched on the sand along the side of the water, frequently resting ourselves, as we were heavily laden. I saw on the sand a number of large fish, that had been left in flat or hollow places; as the wind fell and the waves abated they were left without water, or only a small quantity; and numbers of bald and gray eagles, etc., were along the shore devouring them.

Some time in the afternoon we came to a large camp of Wyandots, at the mouth of Canesadooharie, where Tontileaugo's wife was. Here we were kindly received; they gave us a kind of rough, brown potatoes, which grew spontaneously, and were called by the Caughnewagas *ohnenata.* These potatoes, peeled and dipped in raccoon's fat, taste nearly like our sweet potatoes. They also gave us what they call *canaheanta,* which is a kind of hominy, made of green corn, dried, and beans, mixed together.

We continued our camp at the mouth of Canesadooharie for some time, where we killed some deer and a great many raccoons; the raccoons here were remarkably large and fat. At length we all embarked in a large birch-bark canoe. This vessel was about four feet wide and three feet deep, and about five-and-thirty feet long; and though it could carry a heavy burden, it was so artfully and curiously constructed that four men could carry it several miles, or from one landing-place to another, or from the waters of the lake to the waters of the Ohio. We proceeded up Canesadooharie a few miles, and went on shore to hunt; but, to my great surprise, they carried the vessel we all came in up the bank, and inverted it, or turned the bottom up, and converted it to a dwelling-house, and kindled a fire before us to warm ourselves by and cook. With our baggage and ourselves in this house we were very much crowded, yet our little house turned off the rain very well.

While we remained here I left my pouch with my books in camp, wrapped up in my blanket, and went out to hunt chestnuts. On my return to camp my books were missing. I inquired after them, and asked the Indians if they knew where they were;

they told me that they supposed the puppies had carried them off. I did not believe them, but thought they were displeased at my poring over my books, and concluded that they had destroyed them, or put them out of my way.

After this I was again out after nuts, and on my return beheld a new erection, composed of two white-oak saplings, that were forked about twelve feet high, and stood about fifteen feet apart. They had cut these saplings at the forks, and laid a strong pole across, which appeared in the form of a gallows; and the poles they had shaved very smooth, and painted in places with vermilion. I could not conceive the use of this piece of work, and at length concluded it was a gallows. I thought that I had displeased them by reading my books, and that they were about putting me to death. The next morning I observed them bringing their skins all to this place, and hanging them over this pole, so as to preserve them from being injured by the weather. This removed my fears. They also buried their large canoe in the ground, which is the way they took to preserve this sort of a canoe in the winter season.

As we had at this time no horse, every one got a pack on his back, and we steered an east course about twelve miles and encamped. The next morning we proceeded on the same course about ten miles to a large creek that empties into Lake Erie, betwixt Canesadooharie and Cayahoga. Here they made their winter cabin in the following form: they cut logs about fifteen feet long, and laid these logs upon each other, and drove posts in the ground at each end to keep them together; the posts they tied together at the top with bark, and by this means raised a wall fifteen feet long and about four feet high, and in the same manner they raised another wall opposite to this, at about twelve feet distance; then they drove forks in the ground in the centre of each end, and laid a strong pole from end to end on these forks; and from these walls to the poles they set up poles instead of rafters, and on these they tied small poles in place of laths; and a cover was made of lynn-bark, which will run[2] even in the winter season.

---

[2] Peel.

It was some time in December when we finished this winter-cabin; but when we had got into this comparatively fine lodging another difficulty arose—we had nothing to eat. While I was travelling with Tontileaugo, as was before mentioned, and had plenty of fat venison, bear's meat, and raccoons, I then thought it was hard living without bread or salt; but now I began to conclude that, if I had anything that would banish pinching hunger, and keep soul and body together, I would be content.

While the hunters were all out, exerting themselves to the outmost of their ability, the squaws and boys (in which class I was) were scattered out in the bottoms, hunting red haws, black haws, and hickory nuts. As it was too late in the year we did not succeed in gathering haws, but we had tolerable success in scratching up hickory-nuts from under a light snow, and these we carried with us lest the hunters should not succeed. After our return the hunters came in, who had killed only two small turkeys, which were but little among eight hunters and thirteen squaws, boys, and children; but they were divided with the greatest equity and justice; every one got their equal share.

The next day the hunters turned out again, and killed one deer and three bears. One of the bears was very large and remarkably fat. The hunters carried in meat sufficient to give us all a hearty supper and breakfast. The squaws and all that could carry turned out to bring in meat; every one had their share assigned them, and my load was among the least; yet, not being accustomed to carrying in this way, I got exceedingly weary, and told them my load was too heavy; I must leave part of it and come for it again. They made a halt, and only laughed at me, and took part of my load, and added it to a young squaw's, who had as much before as I carried.

This kind of reproof had a greater tendency to excite me to exert myself in carrying without complaining than if they had whipped me for laziness. After this the hunters held a council, and concluded that they must have horses to carry their loads; and that they would go to war, even in this inclement season, in order to bring in horses.

Tontileaugo wished to be one of those who should go to war; but the votes went against him, as he was one of our best hunters; it was thought necessary to leave him at this winter-camp to provide for the squaws and children. It was agreed upon that Tontileaugo and three others should stay and hunt, and the other four go to war.

They then began to go through their common ceremony. They sung their war-songs, danced their war-dances, etc. And when they were equipped they went off singing their marching-song and firing their guns. Our camp appeared to be rejoicing; but I was grieved to think that some innocent persons would be murdered, not thinking of danger.

After the departure of these warriors we had hard times; and though we were not altogether out of provisions, we were brought to short allowance. At length Tontileaugo had considerable success, and we had meat brought into camp sufficient to last ten days. Tontileaugo then took me with him in order to encamp some distance from this winter-cabin, to try his luck there. We carried no provisions with us; he said he would leave what was there for the squaws and children, and that we could shift for ourselves. We steered about a south course up the waters of this creek, and encamped about ten or twelve miles from the winter-cabin. As it was still cold weather, and a crust upon the snow, which made a noise as we walked, and alarmed the deer, we could kill nothing, and consequently went to sleep without supper. The only chance we had, under these circumstances, was to hunt bear-holes; as the bears, about Christmas, search out a winter lodging-place, where they lie about three or four months without eating or drinking. This may appear to some incredible, but it is well known to be the case by those who live in the remote western parts of North America.

The next morning early we proceeded on, and when we found a tree scratched by the bears climbing up, and the hole in the tree sufficiently large for the reception of the bear, we then felled a sapling or small tree against or near the hole, and it was my business to climb up and drive out the bear, while Tontileaugo stood ready with his gun and bow. We went on in this manner until evening without success. At length we found a large elm scratched, and a hole in it about forty feet up, but no tree nigh suitable to lodge against the hole. Tontileaugo got a long pole and some dry rotten wood, which he tied in bunches with bark; and as there was a tree that grew near the elm, and extended up near the hole, but leaned the wrong way, so that we could not lodge it to advantage, to remedy this inconvenience he climbed up this tree and carried with him his rotten wood, fire, and pole. The rotten wood he tied to his belt, and to one end of the pole he tied a hook and a piece of rotten wood, which he set fire to, as it would retain fire almost like punk, and reached this hook from limb to limb as he went up. When he got up with his pole he put dry wood on fire into the hole; after he put in the fire he heard the bear snuff, and he came speedily down, took his gun in his hand, and waited until the bear would come out; but it was some time before it appeared, and when it did appear he attempted taking sight with his rifle; but it being then too dark to see the sights, he set it down by a tree, and instantly bent his bow, took hold of an arrow, and shot the bear a little behind the shoulder. I was preparing also to shoot an arrow, but he called to me to stop, there was no occasion; and with that the bear fell to the ground.

Being very hungry, we kindled a fire, opened the bear, took out the liver, and wrapped some of the caul-fat round, and put it on a wooden spit, which we stuck in the ground by the fire to roast; then we skinned the bear, got on our kettle, and had both roast and boiled, and also sauce to our meat, which appeared to me to be delicate fare. After I was fully satisfied I went to sleep; Tontileaugo awoke me, saying, "Come, eat hearty, we have got meat plenty now."

The next morning we cut down a lynn-tree, peeled bark and made a snug little shelter, facing the southeast, with a large log betwixt us and the northwest; we made a good fire before us, and scaffolded up our meat at one side. When we had finished our camp we went out to hunt; searched two trees for bears, but to no purpose. As the snow thawed a little in the afternoon, Tontileaugo killed a deer, which we carried with us to camp.

Some time in February the four warriors returned, who had taken two scalps and six horses from the frontiers of Pennsylvania. The hunters could then scatter out a considerable distance from the winter-cabin and encamp, kill meat, and bring it in upon horses; so that we commonly, after this, had plenty of provision.

In this month we began to make sugar. As some of the elm-bark will strip at this season, the squaws, after finding a tree that would do, cut it down, and with a crooked stick, broad and sharp at the end, took the bark off the tree, and of this bark made vessels, in a curious manner, that would hold about two gallons each; they made above one hundred of these kind of vessels. In the sugar-tree they cut a notch, sloping down, and at the end of the notch stuck in a tomahawk; in the place where they stuck the tomahawk they drove a long chip, in order to carry the water out from the tree, and under this they set their vessel to receive it. As sugar-trees were plenty and large here, they seldom or never notched a tree that was not two or three feet over. They also made bark vessels for carrying the water that would hold about four gallons each. They had two brass kettles that held about fifteen gallons each, and other smaller kettles in which they boiled the water. But as they could not at times boil away the water as fast as it was collected, they made vessels of bark that would hold about one hundred gallons each for retaining the water; and though the sugar-trees did not run every day, they had always a sufficient quantity of water to keep them boiling during the whole sugar-season.

About the latter end of March we began to prepare for moving into town in order to plant corn. The squaws were then frying the last of their bear's fat and making vessels to hold it; the vessels were made of deer-skins, which were skinned by pulling the skin off the neck without ripping. After they had taken off the hair they gathered it in small plaits round the neck, and, with a string, drew it together like a purse; in the centre a pin was put, below which they tied a string, and while it was wet they blew it up like a bladder, and let it remain in this manner until it was dry, when it appeared nearly in the shape of a sugar-loaf, but more rounding at the lower end. One of these vessels would hold about four or five gallons. In these vessels it was they carried their bear's oil.

When all things were ready we moved back to the falls of Canesadooharie. On our arrival at the falls (as we had brought with us on horseback about two hundred weight of sugar, a large quantity of bear's oil, skins, etc.) the canoe we had buried was not sufficient to carry all; therefore we were obliged to make another one of elm-bark. While we lay here a young Wyandot found my books. On this they collected together. I was a little way from the camp, and saw the collection, but did not know what it meant. They called me by my Indian name, which was Scoouwa, repeatedly. I ran to see what was the matter; they showed me my books, and said they were glad they had been found, for they knew I was grieved at the loss of them, and that they now rejoiced with me because they were found. As I could then speak some Indian, especially Caughnewaga (for both that and the Wyandot tongue were spoken in this camp), I told them that I thanked them for the kindness they had always shown to me, and also for finding my books. They asked if the books were damaged. I told them not much. They then showed how they lay, which was in the best manner to turn off the water. In a deer-skin pouch they lay all winter. The print was not much injured, though the binding was. This was the first time that I felt my heart warm towards the Indians. Though they had been exceedingly kind to me, I still before detested them on account of the barbarity I beheld after Braddock's defeat. Neither had I ever before pretended kindness, or expressed myself in a friendly manner; but I began now to excuse the Indians on account of their want of information.

We staid at this camp about two weeks, and killed a number of bears, raccoons, and some beavers. We made a canoe of elm-bark, and Tontileaugo embarked in it. He arrived at the falls that night; while I, mounted on horseback, with a bear-skin saddle and bark stirrups, proceeded by land to the falls. I came there the next morning, and we carried our canoe and loading past the falls.

We again proceeded towards the lakes; I on horseback and Tontileaugo by water. Here the land is generally good, but I found some difficulty in getting round swamps and ponds. When we came to the lake I proceeded along the strand and Tontileaugo near the shore, sometimes paddling and sometimes poling his canoe along.

After some time the wind arose, and he went into the mouth of a small creek and encamped. Here we staid several days on account of high wind, which raised the lake in great billows. While we were here Tontileaugo went out to hunt, and when he was gone a Wyandot came to our camp. I gave him a shoulder of venison which I had by the fire well roasted, and he received it gladly; told me he was hungry, and thanked me for my kindness. When Tontileaugo came home I told him that a Wyandot had been at camp, and that I gave him a shoulder of roasted venison. He said that was very well, "and I suppose you gave him also sugar and bear's oil to eat with his venison." I told him I did not, as the sugar and bear's oil were down in the canoe, I did not go for it. He replied, "You have behaved just like a Dutchman.[3] Do you not know that when strangers come to our camp we ought always to give them the best that we have?" I acknowledged that I was wrong. He said that he could excuse this, as I was but young; but I must learn to behave like a warrior, and do great things, and never be found in any such little actions.

The lake being again calm, we proceeded, and arrived safe at Sunyendeand, which was a Wyandot town that lay upon a small creek which empties into the little lake below the mouth of Sandusky.

The town was about eighty rood above the mouth of the creek, on the south side of a large plain, on which timber grew, and nothing more but grass or nettles. In some places there were large flats where nothing but grass grew, about three feet high when grown, and in other places nothing but nettles, very rank, where the soil is extremely rich and loose; here they planted corn. In this town there were also French traders, who purchased our skins and fur, and we all got new clothes, paint, tobacco, etc.

After I had got my new clothes, and my head done off like a red-headed woodpecker, I, in company with a number of young Indians, went down to the corn-field to see the squaws at work. When we came there they asked me to take a hoe, which I did, and hoed for some time. The squaws applauded me as a good hand at the business; but when I returned to the town the old men, hearing of what I had done, chid me, and said that I was adopted in the place of a great man, and must not hoe corn like

---

[3] The Dutch he called Skoharehaugo, which took its derivation from a Dutch settlement called Skoharey.

a squaw. They never had occasion to reprove me for anything like this again; as I never was extremely fond of work, I readily complied with their orders.

As the Indians, on their return from their winter hunt, bring in with them large quantities of bear's oil, sugar, dried venison, etc., at this time they have plenty, and do not spare eating or giving; thus they make way with their provision as quick as possible. They have no such thing as regular meals, breakfast, dinner, or supper; but if any one, even the town-folks, would go to the same house several times in one day, he would be invited to eat of the best; and with them it is bad manners to refuse to eat when it is offered. If they will not eat it is interpreted as a symptom of displeasure, or that the persons refusing to eat were angry with those who had invited them.

At this time hominy, plentifully mixed with bear's oil and sugar, or dried venison, bear's oil, and sugar, is what they offer to every one who comes in any time of the day; and so they go on until their sugar, bear's oil, and venison are all gone, and then they have to eat hominy by itself, without bread, salt, or anything else; yet still they invite every one that comes in to eat while they have anything to give. It is thought a shame not to invite people to eat while they have anything; but if they can in truth only say we have got nothing to eat, this is accepted as an honorable apology. All the hunters and warriors continued in town about six weeks after we came in; they spent this time in painting, going from house to house, eating, smoking, and playing at a game resembling dice, or hustle-cap. They put a number of plum-stones in a small bowl; one side of each stone is black, and the other white; they then shake or hustle the bowl, calling, "*Hits, hits, hits, honesey, honesey, rago, rago;*" which signifies calling for white or black, or what they wish to turn up; they then turn the bowl, and count the whites and blacks. Some were beating their kind of drum and singing; others were employed in playing on a sort of flute made of hollow cane; and others playing on the jew's-harp. Some part of this time was also taken up in attending the council-house, where the chiefs, and as many others as chose, attended; and at night they were frequently employed in singing and dancing. Towards the last of this time, which was in June, 1756, they were all engaged in preparing to go to war against the frontiers of Virginia. When they were equipped they went through their ceremonies, sung their war-songs, etc. They all marched off, from fifteen to sixty years of age; and some boys, only twelve years of age, were equipped with their bows and arrows, and went to war; so that none were left in town but squaws and children, except myself, one very old man, and another, about fifty years of age, who was lame.

The Indians were then in great hopes that they would drive all the Virginians over the lake, which is all the name they know for the sea. When the warriors left this town we had neither meat, sugar, or bear's oil left. All that we had then to live on was corn pounded into coarse meal or small hominy; this they boiled in water, which appeared like well-thickened soup, without salt or anything else. For some time we had plenty of this kind of hominy; at length we were brought to very short allowance, and as the warriors did not return as soon as they expected, we were soon in a starving condition, and but one gun in the town, and very little ammunition. The old lame Wyandot concluded that he would go a-hunting in a canoe, and take me with him, and try to kill deer in the water, as it was then watering time. We went up Sandusky a few miles, then turned up a creek and encamped. We had lights prepared, as we were to hunt in the night, and also a piece of bark and some bushes set up in the canoe, in order to conceal ourselves from the deer. A little boy that was with us held the light; I worked the canoe, and the old man, who had his gun loaded with large shot, when we came near the deer, fired, and in this manner killed three deer in part of one night. We went to our fire, ate heartily, and in the morning returned to town in order to relieve the hungry and distressed.

When we came to town the children were crying bitterly on account of pinching hunger. We delivered what we had taken, and though it was but little among so many, it was divided according to the strictest rules of justice. We immediately set out for another hunt, but before we returned a part of the warriors had come in, and brought with them on horseback a quantity of meat. These warriors had divided into different parties, and all struck at different places in Augusta County. They brought in with them a considerable number of scalps, prisoners, horses, and other plunder. One of the parties brought in with them one Arthur Campbell, that is now Colonel Campbell, who lives on Holston River, near the Royal Oak. As the Wyandots at Sunyendeand and those at Detroit were connected, Mr. Campbell was taken to Detroit; but he remained some time with me in this town. His company was very agreeable, and I was sorry when he left me. During his stay at Sunyendeand he borrowed my Bible, and made some pertinent remarks on what he had read. One passage was where it is said, "It is good for a man that he bear the yoke in his youth." He said we ought to be resigned to the will of Providence, as we were now bearing the yoke in our youth. Mr. Campbell appeared to be then about sixteen or seventeen years of age.

About the time that these warriors came in the green corn was beginning to be of use, so that we had either green corn or venison, and sometimes both, which was, comparatively, high living. When we could have plenty of green corn, or roasting ears, the hunters became lazy, and spent their time, as already mentioned, in singing and dancing, etc. They appeared to be fulfilling the Scriptures beyond those who profess to believe in them, in that of taking no thought of to-morrow; and also in living in love, peace, and friendship together, without disputes. In this respect they shame those who profess Christianity.

In this manner we lived until October; then the geese, swans, ducks, cranes, etc., came from the north, and alighted on this little lake, without number, or innumerable. Sunyendeand is a remarkable place for fish in the spring, and fowl both in the fall and spring.

As our hunters were now tired with indolence, and fond of their own kind of exercise, they all turned out to fowling, and in this could scarce miss of success; so that we had now plenty of hominy and the best of fowls; and sometimes, as a rarity, we had a little bread, which was made of Indian-corn meal, pounded in a hominy block, mixed with boiled beans, and baked in cakes under the ashes.

This with us was called good living, though not equal to our fat, roasted, and boiled venison, when we went to the woods in the fall; or bear's meat and beaver in the winter; or sugar, bear's oil, and dry venison in the spring.

Some time in October, another adopted brother, older than Tontileaugo came to pay us a visit at Sunyendeand, and he asked me to take a hunt with him on Cayahoga. As they always used me as a free man, and gave me the liberty of choosing, I told him that I was attached to Tontileaugo, had never seen him before, and therefore asked some time to consider of this. He told me that the party he was going with would not be along, or at the mouth of this little lake, in less than six days, and I could in this time be acquainted with him, and judge for myself. I consulted with Tontileaugo on this occasion, and he told me that our old brother Tecaughretanego (which was his name) was a chief, and a better man than he was, and if I went with him I might expect to be well used; but he said I might do as I pleased, and if I staid he would use me as he had done. I told him that he had acted in every respect as a brother to me; yet I was much pleased with my old brother's conduct and conversation; and as he was going to a part of the country I had never been in, I wished to go with him. He said that he was perfectly willing.

I then went with Tecaughretanego to the mouth of the little lake, where he met with the company he intended going with, which was composed of Caughnewagas and Ottawas. As the wind was high and we could not proceed on our voyage, we remained here several days, and killed abundance of wild fowl, and a number of raccoons.

When a company of Indians are moving together on the lake, as it is at this time of the year often dangerous sailing, the old men hold a council; and when they agree to embark, every one is engaged immediately in making ready, without offering one word against the measure, though the lake may be boisterous and horrid. One morning, though the wind appeared to me to be as high as in days past, and the billows raging, yet the call was given *"yohoh-yohoh,"* which was quickly answered by all— *"ooh-ooh,"* which signifies agreed. We were all instantly engaged in preparing to start, and had considerable difficulties in embarking.

As soon as we got into our canoes we fell to paddling with all our might, making out from the shore. Though these sort of canoes ride waves beyond what could be expected, yet the water several times dashed into them. When we got out about half a mile from shore we hoisted sail, and as it was nearly a west wind, we then seemed to ride the waves with ease, and went on at a rapid rate. We then all laid down our paddles, excepting one that steered, and there was no water dashed into our canoes until we came near the shore again. We sailed about sixty miles that day, and encamped some time before night.

The next day we again embarked, and went on very well for some time; but the lake being boisterous, and the wind not fair, we were obliged to make to shore, which we accomplished with hard work and some difficulty in landing. The next morning a council was held by the old men.

As we had this day to pass by a long precipice of rocks on the shore, about nine miles, which rendered it impossible for us to land, though the wind was high and the lake rough, yet, as it was fair, we were all ordered to embark. We wrought ourselves out from the shore and hoisted sail (what we used in place of sail-cloth were our tent-mats, which answered the purpose very well), and went on for some time with a fair wind, until we were opposite to the precipice, and then it turned towards the shore, and we began to fear we should be cast upon the rocks. Two of the canoes were considerably farther out from the rocks than the canoe I was in. Those who were farthest out in the lake did not let down their sails until they had passed the precipice; but as we were nearer the rock, we were obliged to lower our sails, and paddle with all our might. With much difficulty we cleared ourselves of the rock, and landed. As the other canoes had landed before us, there were immediately runners sent off to see if we were all safely landed.

About the first of December, 1756, we were preparing for leaving the river: we buried our canoes, and as usual hung up our skins, and every one had a pack to carry. The squaws also packed up their tents, which they carried in large rolls that extended up above their heads, and though a great bulk, yet not heavy. We steered about a southeast course, and could not march over ten miles per day. At night we lodged in our flag tents, which, when erected, were nearly in the shape of a sugar-loaf, and about fifteen feet diameter at the ground.

In this manner we proceeded about forty miles, and wintered in these tents, on the waters of Beaver Creek, near a little lake or large pond, which is about two miles long and one broad, and a remarkable place for beaver.

It is a received opinion among Indians that the geese turn to beavers, and the snakes to raccoons; and though Tecaughretanego, who was a wise man, was not fully persuaded that this was true, yet he seemed in some measure to be carried away with this whimsical notion. He said that this pond had been always a great place for beaver. Though he said he knew them to be frequently all killed (as he thought), yet the next winter they would be as plenty as ever. And as the beaver was an animal that did not travel by land, and there being no water communication to or from this pond, how could such a number of beavers get there year after year? But as this pond was also a considerable place for geese, when they came in the fall from the north, and alighted in this pond, they turned beavers, all but the feet, which remained nearly the same.

In conversation with Tecaughretanego I happened to be talking of the beavers catching fish. He asked me why I thought that the beaver caught fish. I told him that I had read of the beaver making dams for the conveniency of fishing. He laughed, and made game of me and my book. He said the man that wrote that book knew nothing about the beaver. The beaver never did eat flesh of any kind, but lived on the bark of trees, roots, and other vegetables.

In order to know certainly how this was, when we killed a beaver I carefully examined the intestines, but found no appearance of fish; I afterwards made an experiment on a pet beaver which we had, and found that it would neither eat fish nor flesh; therefore I acknowledged that the book I had read was wrong.

Near this pond beaver was the principal game. Before the water froze up we caught a great many with wooden and steel traps; but after that we hunted the beaver on the ice. Some places here the beavers build large houses to live in; and in other places they have subterraneous lodgings in the banks. Where they lodge in the ground we have no chance of hunting them on the ice; but where they have houses, we go with mauls and handspikes, and break all the hollow ice, to prevent them from getting their heads above the water under it. Then we break a hole in the house, and they make their escape into the water; but as they cannot live long under water, they are obliged to go to some of those broken places to breathe, and the Indians commonly put in their hands, catch them by the hind-leg, haul them on the ice, and tomahawk them. Sometimes they shoot them in the head when they raise it above the water. I asked the Indians if they were not afraid to catch the beavers with their hands. They said no: they were not much of a biting creature; yet if they would catch them by the fore-foot they would bite.

I went out with Tecaughretanego and some others a beaver hunting; but we did not succeed, and on our return we saw where several raccoons had passed while the snow was soft, though there was now a crust upon it; we all made a halt, looking at the raccoon tracks. As they saw a tree with a hole in it, they told me to go and see if they had gone in thereat; and if they had to halloo, and they would come and take them out. When I went to that tree, I found they had gone past; but I saw another the way they had gone, and proceeded to examine that, and found they had gone up it. I then began to halloo, but could have no answer.

As it began to snow and blow most violently, I returned and proceeded after my company, and for some time could see their tracks; but the old snow being only about three inches deep, and a crust upon it, the present driving snow soon filled up the tracks. As I had only a bow, arrows, and tomahawk with me, and no way to strike fire, I appeared to be in a dismal situation; and as the air was dark with snow, I had little more prospect of steering my course than I would in the night. At length I came to a hollow tree, with a hole at one side that I could go in at. I went in, and found that it was a dry place, and the hollow about three feet diameter, and high enough for me to stand in. I found that there was also a considerable quantity of soft, dry rotten wood around this hollow; I therefore concluded that I would lodge here, and that I would go to work, and stop up the door of my house. I stripped off my blanket (which was all the clothes that I had, excepting a breech-clout, leggings, and moccasons), and with my tomahawk fell to chopping at the top of a fallen tree that lay near, and carried wood, and set it up on end against the door, until I had it three or four feet thick all around, excepting a hole I had left to creep in at. I had a block prepared that I could haul after me to stop this hole; and before I went in I put in a number of small sticks that I might more effectually stop it on the inside. When I went in, I took my tomahawk and cut down all the dry rotten wood I could get, and beat it small. With it I made a bed like a goose-nest or hog-bed, and with the small sticks stopped every hole, until my house was almost dark. I stripped off my moccasons, and danced in the centre of my bed, for half an hour, in order to warm myself. In this time my feet and whole body were agreeably warmed. The snow, in the meanwhile, had stopped all the holes, so that my house was as dark as a dungeon, though I knew it could not yet be dark out of doors. I then coiled myself up in my blanket, lay down in my little round bed, and had a tolerable night's lodging. When I awoke all was dark—not the least glimmering of light was to be seen. Immediately I recollected that I was not to expect light in this new habitation, as there was neither door nor window in it. As I could hear the storm raging, and did not suffer much cold as I was then situated, I concluded I would stay in my nest until I was certain it was day. When I had reason to conclude that it surely was day, I arose and put on my moccasons, which I had laid under my head to keep from freezing. I then endeavored to find the door, and had to do all by the sense of feeling, which took me some time. At length I found the block, but it being heavy, and a large quantity of snow having fallen on it, at the first attempt I did not move it. I then felt terrified—among all the hardships I had sustained, I never knew before what it was to be thus deprived of light. This, with the other circumstances attending it, appeared grievous. I went straightway to bed again, wrapped my blanket round me, and lay and mused awhile, and then prayed to Almighty God to direct and protect me as he had done heretofore. I once again attempted to move away the block, which proved successful; it moved about nine inches. With this a considerable quantity of snow fell in from above, and I immediately received light; so that I found a very great snow had fallen, above what I had ever seen in one night. I then knew why I could not easily move the block, and I was so rejoiced at obtaining the light that all my other difficulties seemed to vanish. I then turned into my cell, and returned God thanks for having once more received the light of heaven. At length I belted my blanket about me, got my tomahawk, bow and arrows, and went out of my den.

I was now in tolerable high spirits, though the snow had fallen above three feet deep, in addition to what was on the ground before; and the only imperfect guide I had in order to steer my course to camp was the trees, as the moss generally grows on the northwest side of them, if they are straight. I proceeded on, wading through the snow, and about twelve o'clock (as it appeared afterwards, from that time to night, for it was yet cloudy) I came upon the creek that our camp was on, about half a mile below the camp; and when I came in sight of the camp I found that there was great joy, by the shouts and yelling of the boys, etc.

When I arrived they all came round me, and received me gladly; but at this time no questions were asked, and I was taken into a tent, where they gave me plenty of fat beaver meat, and then asked me to smoke. When I had done, Tecaughretanego desired me to walk out to a fire they had made. I went out, and they all collected round me, both men, women, and boys. Tecaughretanego asked me to give them a particular account of what had happened from the time they left me yesterday until now. I told them the whole of the story, and they never interrupted me; but when I made a stop, the intervals were filled with loud exclamations of joy. As I could not at this time talk Ottawa or Jibewa well (which is nearly the same), I delivered my story in Caughnewaga. As my sister Molly's husband was a Jibewa, and could understand Caughnewaga, he acted as interpreter, and delivered my story to the Jibewas and Ottawas, which they received with pleasure.

One day, as I was looking after my traps, I got benighted, by beaver ponds intercepting my way to camp; and as I had neglected to take fireworks with me, and the weather very cold, I could find no suitable lodging-place; therefore the only expedient I could think of to keep myself from freezing was exercise. I danced and hallooed the whole night with all my might, and the next day came to camp. Though I suffered much more this time than the other night I lay out, yet the Indians were not so much concerned, as they thought I had fireworks with me; but when they knew how it was, they did not blame me. They said that old hunters were frequently involved in this place, as the beaver dams were one above another on every creek and run, so that it is hard to find a fording-place. They applauded me for my fortitude, and said, as they had now plenty of beaver skins, they would purchase me a new gun at Detroit, as we were to go there the next spring; and then if I should chance to be lost in dark weather, I could make a fire, kill provision, and return to camp when the sun shone. By being bewildered on the waters of Muskingum, I lost repute, and was reduced to the bow and arrow, and by lying out two nights here I regained my credit.

After some time the waters all froze again, and then, as formerly, we hunted beavers on the ice. Though beaver meat, without salt or bread, was the chief of our food this winter, yet we had always plenty, and I was well contented with my diet, as it appeared delicious fare after the way we had lived the winter before.

Some time in February we scaffolded up our fur and skins, and moved about ten miles in quest of a sugar-camp, or a suitable place to make sugar, and encamped in a large bottom on the head-waters of Big Beaver Creek. We had some difficulty in moving, as we had a blind Caughnewaga boy, about fifteen years of age, to lead; and as this country is very brushy, we frequently had him to carry. We had also my Jibewa brother-in-law's father with us, who was thought by the Indians to be a great conjuror; his name was Manetohcoa. This old man was so decrepit that we had to carry him this route upon a bier, and all our baggage to pack on our backs.

Some time in March, 1757, we began to move back to the forks of Cayahoga, which was about forty or fifty miles. And as we had no horses, we had all our baggage and several hundred weight of beaver skins, and some deer and bear skins, all to pack on our backs. The method we took to accomplish this was by making short days' journeys. In the morning we would move on with as much as we were able to carry, about five miles, and encamp, and then run back for more. We commonly made three such trips in the day. When we came to the great pond, we staid there one day to rest ourselves, and to kill ducks and geese.

When we came to the forks, we found that the skins we had scaffolded were all safe. Though this was a public place, and Indians frequently passing, and our skins hanging up in view, yet there were none stolen. And it is seldom that Indians do steal anything from one another. And they say they never did, until the white people came among them, and taught some of them to lie, cheat, and steal; but be that as it may, they never did curse or swear until the whites taught them. Some think their language will not admit of it, but I am not of that opinion. If I was so disposed, I could find language to curse or swear in the Indian tongue.

We took up our birch-bark canoes which we had buried, and found that they were not damaged by the winter; but they not being sufficient to carry all that we now had, we made a large chestnut-bark canoe, as elm-bark was not to be found at this place.

We all embarked, and had a very agreeable passage down the Cayahoga, and along the south side of Lake Erie, until we passed the mouth of Sandusky; then the wind arose, and we put in at the mouth of the Miami of the Lake, at Cedar Point, where we remained several days, and killed a number of turkeys, geese, ducks, and swans. The wind being fair, and the lake not extremely rough, we again embarked, hoisted up sails, and arrived safe at the Wyandot town, nearly opposite to Fort Detroit, on the north side of the river. Here we found a number of French traders, every one very willing to deal with us for our beaver.

We bought ourselves fine clothes, ammunition, paint, tobacco, etc., and, according to promise, they purchased me a new gun; yet we had parted with only about one third of our beaver. At length a trader came to town with French brandy; we purchased a keg of it, and held a council about who was to get drunk and who was to keep sober. I was invited to get drunk, but I refused the proposal; then they told me that I must be one of those who were to take care of the drunken people. I did not like this; but of two evils I chose that which I thought was the least—and fell in with those who were to conceal the arms, and keep every dangerous weapon we could out of their way, and endeavor, if possible, to keep the drinking-club from killing each other, which was a very hard task. Several times we hazarded our own lives, and got ourselves hurt in preventing them from slaying each other. Before they had finished this keg, near one third of the town was introduced to this drinking-club; they could not pay their part, as they had already disposed of all their skins; but that made no odds—all were welcome to drink. When they were done with this keg, they applied to the traders, and procured a kettle full of brandy at a time, which they divided out with a large wooden spoon; and so they went on, and never quit while they had a single beaver skin. When the trader had got all our beaver, he moved off to the Ottawa town, about a mile above the Wyandot town.

When the brandy was gone, and the drinking-club sober, they appeared much dejected. Some of them were crippled, others badly wounded, a number of their fine new shirts torn, and several blankets were burned. A number of squaws were also in this club, and neglected their corn-planting. We could now hear the effects of the brandy in the Ottawa town. They were singing and yelling in the most hideous manner, both night and day; but their frolic ended worse than ours: five Ottawas were killed and a great many wounded.

After this a number of young Indians were getting their ears cut, and they urged me to have mine cut likewise, but they did not attempt to compel me, though they endeavored to persuade me. The principal arguments they used were, its being a very great ornament, and also the common fashion. The former I did not believe, and the latter I could not deny. The way they performed this operation was by cutting the fleshy part of the circle of the ear, close to the gristle, quite through. When this was done they wrapped rags round this fleshy part until it was entirely healed; they then hung lead to it, and stretched it to a wonderful length: when it was sufficiently stretched, they wrapped the fleshy part round with brass wire, which formed it into a semicircle about four inches in diameter.

Many of the young men were now exercising themselves in a game resembling football, though they commonly struck the ball with a crooked stick made for that purpose; also a game something like this, wherein they used a wooden ball, about three inches in diameter, and the instrument they moved it with was a strong staff, about five feet long, with a hoop net on the end of it large enough to contain the ball. Before they begin the play, they lay off about half a mile distance in a clear plain, and the opposite parties all attend at the centre, where a disinterested person casts up the ball, then the opposite parties all contend for it. If any one gets it into his net, he runs with it the way he wishes it to go, and they all pursue him. If one of the opposite party overtakes the person with the ball, he gives the staff a stroke, which causes the ball to fly out of the net; then they have another debate for it, and if the one that gets it can outrun all the opposite party, and can carry it quite out, or over the line at the end, the game is won; but this seldom happens. When any one is running away with the ball, and is likely to be overtaken, he commonly throws it, and with this instrument can cast it fifty or sixty yards. Sometimes when the ball is almost at the one end, matters will take a sudden turn, and the opposite party may quickly carry it out at the other end. Oftentimes they will work a long while back and forward before they can get the ball over the line, or win the game.

About the 1st of June, 1757, the warriors were preparing to go to war, in the Wyandot, Pottowatomy, and Ottawa towns; also a great many Jibewas came down from the upper lakes; and after singing their war-songs and going through their common ceremonies, they marched off against the frontiers of Virginia, Maryland, and Pennsylvania, in their usual manner, singing the travelling song, slow firing, etc.

About the middle of June the Indians were almost all gone to war, from sixteen to sixty; yet Tecaughretanego remained in town with me. Though he had formerly, when they were at war with the southern nations, been a great warrior and an eminent counsellor, and I think as clear and able a reasoner upon any subject that he had an opportunity of being acquainted with as I ever knew, yet he had all along been against this war, and had strenuously opposed it in council. He said, if the English and French had a quarrel, let them fight their own battles themselves; it is not our business to intermeddle therewith.

Before the warriors returned we were very scarce of provision; and though we did not commonly steal from one another, yet we stole during this time anything that we could eat from the French, under the notion that it was just for us to do so, because they supported their soldiers; and our squaws, old men, and children were suffering on account of the war, as our hunters were all gone.

Some time in August the warriors returned, and brought in with them a great many scalps, prisoners, horses, and plunder; and the common report among the young warriors was that they would entirely subdue Tulhasaga, that is the English, or it might be literally rendered the Morning Light Inhabitants.

About the first of November a number of families were preparing to go on their winter hunt, and all agreed to cross the lake together. We encamped at the mouth of the river the first night, and a council was held, whether we should cross through by the three islands, or coast it round the lake. These islands lie in a line across the lake, and are just in sight of each other. Some of the Wyandots, or Ottawas, frequently make their winter hunt on these islands; though, excepting wild fowl and fish, there is scarcely any game here but raccoons, which are amazingly plenty, and exceedingly large and fat, as they feed upon the wild rice, which grows in abundance in wet places round these islands. It is said that each hunter, in one winter, will catch one thousand raccoons.

It is a received opinion among the Indians that the snakes and raccoons are transmigratory, and that a great many of the snakes turn into raccoons every fall, and raccoons into snakes every spring. This notion is founded on observations made on the snakes and raccoons in this island.

We concluded to coast it round the lake, and in two days we came to the mouth of the Miami of the Lake, and landed on Cedar Point, where we remained several days. Here we held a council, and concluded we would take a driving hunt in concert and in partnership.

The river in this place is about a mile broad, and as it and the lake form a kind of neck, which terminates in a point, all the hunters (which were fifty-three) went up the river, and we scattered ourselves from the river to the lake. When we first began to move we were not in sight of each other, but as we all raised the yell, we could move regularly together by the noise. At length we came in sight of each other, and appeared to be marching in good order; before we came to the point, both the squaws and boys in the canoes were scattered up the river and along the lake, to prevent the deer from making their escape by water. As we advanced near the point the guns began to crack slowly, and after some time the firing was like a little engagement. The squaws and boys were busy tomahawking the deer in the water, and we shooting them down on the land. We killed in all about thirty deer, though a great many made their escape by water.

Here our company separated. The chief part of them went up the Miami River,[4] which empties into Lake Erie at Cedar Point, while we proceeded on our journey in company with Tecaughretanego, Tontileaugo, and two families of the Wyandots.

As cold weather was now approaching, we began to feel the doleful effects of extravagantly and foolishly spending the large quantity of beaver we had taken in our last winter's hunt. We were all nearly in the same circumstances; scarcely one had a shirt to his back; but each of us had an old blanket which we belted round us in the day, and slept in at night, with a deer or bear skin under us for our bed.

When we came to the Falls of Sandusky we buried our birch-bark canoes, as usual, at a large burying-place for that purpose, a little below the falls. At this place the river falls about eight feet over a rock, but not perpendicularly. With much difficulty we pushed up our wooden canoes; some of us went up the river, and the rest by land with the horses, until we came to the great meadows or prairies that lie between Sandusky and Sciota.

When we came to this place, we met with some Ottawa hunters, and agreed with them to take what they call a ring hunt, in partnership. We waited until we expected rain was near falling to extinguish the fire, and then we kindled a large circle in the prairie. At this time, or before the bucks began to run, a great number of deer lay concealed in the grass in the day, and

---

[4] The Miami of the Lakes, now called Maumee.

moved about in the night; but as the fire burned in towards the centre of the circle, the deer fled before the fire; the Indians were scattered also at some distance before the fire, and shot them down every opportunity, which was very frequent, especially as the circle became small. When we came to divide the deer, there were about ten to each hunter, which were all killed in a few hours. The rain did not come on that night to put out the outside circle of the fire, and as the wind arose, it extended through the whole prairie, which was about fifty miles in length, and in some places nearly twenty in breadth. This put an end to our ring hunting this season, and was in other respects an injury to us in the hunting business; so that upon the whole we received more harm than benefit by our rapid hunting frolic. We then moved from the north end of the glades, and encamped at the carrying-place.

About the time the bucks quit running, Tontileaugo, his wife and children, Tecaughretanego, his son Nunganey, and myself, left the Wyandot camps at the carrying-place, and crossed the Sciota River at the south end of the glades, and proceeded on about a southwest course to a large creek called Ollentangy, which I believe interlocks with the waters of the Miami, and empties into Sciota on the west side thereof. From the south end of the prairie to Ollentangy there is a large quantity of beech land, intermixed with first-rate land. Here we made our winter hut, and had considerable success in hunting.

After some time one of Tontileaugo's stepsons (a lad about eight years of age) offended him, and he gave the boy a moderate whipping, which much displeased his Wyandot wife. She acknowledged that the boy was guilty of a fault, but thought that he ought to have been ducked, which is their usual mode of chastisement. She said she could not bear to have her son whipped like a servant or slave; and she was so displeased, that when Tontileaugo went out to hunt, she got her two horses, and all her effects (as in this country the husband and wife have separate interests), and moved back to the Wyandot camp that we had left.

When Tontileaugo returned he was much disturbed on hearing of his wife's elopement, and said that he would never go after her, were it not that he was afraid that she would get bewildered, and that his children that she had taken with her might suffer. Tontileaugo went after his wife, and when they met they made up the quarrel; and he never returned, but left Tecaughretanego and his son (a boy about ten years of age), and myself, who remained here in our hut all winter.

Tecaughretanego had been a first-rate warrior, statesman, and hunter, and though he was now near sixty years of age, was yet equal to the common run of hunters, but subject to the rheumatism, which deprived him of the use of his legs.

Shortly after Tontileaugo left us, Tecaughretanego became lame, and could scarcely walk out of our hut for two months. I had considerable success in hunting and trapping. Though Tecaughretanego endured much pain and misery, yet he bore it all with wonderful patience, and would often endeavor to entertain me with cheerful conversation. Sometimes he would applaud me for my diligence, skill, and activity; and at other times he would take great care in giving me instructions concerning the hunting and trapping business. He would also tell me that if I failed of success we would suffer very much, as we were about forty miles from any one living, that we knew of; yet he would not intimate that he apprehended we were in any danger, but still supposed that I was fully adequate to the task.

Tontileaugo left us a little before Christmas, and from that until some time in February we had always plenty of bear meat, venison, etc. During this time I killed much more than we could use; but having no horses to carry in what I killed, I left part of it in the woods. In February there came a snow, with a crust, which made a great noise when walking on it, and frightened away the deer; and as bear and beaver were scarce here, we got entirely out of provision. After I had hunted two days without eating anything, and had very short allowance for some days before, I returned late in the evening, faint and weary. When I came into our hut, Tecaughretanego asked what success. I told him not any. He asked me if I was not very hungry. I replied that the keen appetite seemed to be in some measure removed, but I was both faint and weary. He commanded Nunganey, his little son, to bring me something to eat, and he brought me a kettle with some bones and broth. After eating a few mouthfuls, my appetite violently returned, and I thought the victuals had a most agreeable relish, though it was only fox and wildcat bones, which lay about the camp, which the ravens and turkey-buzzards had picked; these Nunganey had collected and boiled, until the sinews that remained on the bones would strip off. I speedily finished my allowance, such as it was, and when I had ended my *sweet* repast, Tecaughretanego asked me how I felt. I told him that I was much refreshed. He then handed me his pipe and pouch, and told me to take a smoke. I did so. He then said he had something of importance to tell me, if I was now composed and ready to hear it. I told him that I was ready to hear him. He said the reason why he deferred his speech till now was because few men are in a right humour to hear good talk when they are extremely hungry, as they are then generally fretful and discomposed; "But as you appear now to enjoy calmness and serenity of mind, I will now communicate to you the thoughts of my heart, and those things that I know to be true.

"*Brother*,—As you have lived with the white people, you have not had the same advantage of knowing that the great Being above feeds his people, and gives them their meat in due season, as we Indians have, who are frequently out of provisions, and yet are wonderfully supplied, and that so frequently, that it is evidently the hand of the great Owaneeyo[5] that doth this. Whereas the white people have commonly large stocks of tame cattle, that they can kill when they please, and also their barns and cribs filled with grain, and therefore have not the same opportunity of seeing and knowing that they are supported by the Ruler of heaven and earth.

"*Brother*,—I know that you are now afraid that we will all perish with hunger, but you have no just reason to fear this.

"*Brother*,—I have been young, but now am old; I have been frequently under the like circumstances that we are now, and that some time or other in almost every year of my life; yet I have hitherto been supported, and my wants supplied in time of need.

"*Brother*,—Owaneeyo sometimes suffers us to be in want, in order to teach us our dependence upon him, and to let us know

---

[5] This is the name of God, in their tongue, and signifies the owner and ruler of all things.

that we are to love and serve him; and likewise to know the worth of the favors that we receive, and to make us more thankful.

"*Brother,*—Be assured that you will be supplied with food, and that just in the right time; but you must continue diligent in the use of means. Go to sleep, and rise early in the morning and go a-hunting; be strong, and exert yourself like a man, and the Great Spirit will direct your way."

The next morning I went out, and steered about an east course. I proceeded on slowly for about five miles, and saw deer frequently; but as the crust on the snow made a great noise, they were always running before I spied them, so that I could not get a shot. A violent appetite returned, and I became intolerably hungry. It was now that I concluded I would run off to Pennsylvania, my native country. As the snow was on the ground, and Indian hunters almost the whole of the way before me, I had but a poor prospect of making my escape, but my case appeared desperate. If I staid here, I thought I would perish with hunger, and if I met with Indians they could but kill me.

I then proceeded on as fast as I could walk, and when I got about ten or twelve miles from our hut I came upon fresh buffalo tracks; I pursued after, and in a short time came in sight of them as they were passing through a small glade. I ran with all my might and headed them, were I lay in ambush, and killed a very large cow. I immediately kindled a fire and began to roast meat, but could not wait till it was done; I ate it almost raw. When hunger was abated I began to be tenderly concerned for my old Indian brother and the little boy I had left in a perishing condition. I made haste and packed up what meat I could carry, secured what I left from the wolves, and returned homewards.

I scarcely thought on the old man's speech while I was almost distracted with hunger, but on my return was much affected with it, reflected on myself for my hard-heartedness and ingratitude, in attempting to run off and leave the venerable old man and little boy to perish with hunger. I also considered how remarkably the old man's speech had been verified in our providentially obtaining a supply. I thought also of that part of his speech which treated of the fractious dispositions of hungry people, which was the only excuse I had for my base inhumanity, in attempting to leave them in the most deplorable situation.

As it was moonlight, I got home to our hut, and found the old man in his usual good-humor. He thanked me for my exertion, and bid me sit down, as I must certainly be fatigued, and he commanded Nunganey to make haste and cook. I told him I would cook for him, and let the boy lay some meat on the coals for himself; which he did, but ate it almost raw, as I had done. I immediately hung on the kettle with some water, and cut the beef in thin slices, and put them in. When it had boiled awhile, I proposed taking it off the fire, but the old man replied, "Let it be done enough." This he said in as patient and unconcerned a manner as if he had not wanted one single meal. He commanded Nunganey to eat no more beef at that time, lest he might hurt himself, but told him to sit down, and after some time he might sup some broth; this command he reluctantly obeyed.

When we were all refreshed, Tecaughretanego delivered a speech upon the necessity and pleasure of receiving the necessary supports of life with thankfulness, knowing that Owaneeyo is the great giver. Such speeches from an Indian may be thought by those who are unacquainted with them altogether incredible; but when we reflect on the Indian war, we may readily conclude that they are not an ignorant or stupid sort of people, or they would not have been such fatal enemies. When they came into our country they outwitted us; and when we sent armies into their country, they outgeneralled and beat us with inferior force. Let us also take into consideration that Tecaughretanego was no common person, but was among the Indians as Socrates in the ancient heathen world; and, it may be, equal to him, if not in wisdom and in learning, yet perhaps in patience and fortitude. Notwithstanding Tecaughretanego's uncommon natural abilities, yet in the sequel of this history you will see the deficiency of the light of nature, unaided by revelation, in this truly great man.

The next morning Tecaughretanego desired me to go back and bring another load of buffalo beef. As I proceeded to do so, about five miles from our hut I found a bear tree. As a sapling grew near the tree, and reached near the hole that the bear went in at, I got dry dozed or rotten wood, that would catch and hold fire almost as well as spunk. This wood I tied up in bunches, fixed them on my back, and then climbed up the sapling, and with a pole I put them, touched with fire, into the hole, and then came down and took my gun in my hand. After some time the bear came out, and I killed and skinned it, packed up a load of the meat (after securing the remainder from the wolves), and returned home before night. On my return my old brother and his son were much rejoiced at my success. After this we had plenty of provisions.

We remained here until some time in April, 1758. At this time Tecaughretanego had recovered so that he could walk about. We made a bark canoe, embarked, and went down Ollentangy some distance, but, the water being low, we were in danger of splitting our canoe upon the rocks; therefore Tecaughretanego concluded we would encamp on shore, and pray for rain.

When we encamped Tecaughretanego made himself a sweat-house, which he did by sticking a number of hoops in the ground, each hoop forming a semicircle; this he covered all round with blankets and skins. He then prepared hot stones, which he rolled into this hut, and then went into it himself with a little kettle of water in his hand, mixed with a variety of herbs, which he had formerly cured, and had now with him in his pack; they afforded an odoriferous perfume. When he was in, he told me to pull down the blankets behind him, and cover all up close, which I did, and then he began to pour water upon the hot stones, and to sing aloud. He continued in this vehement hot place about fifteen minutes. All this he did in order to purify himself before he would address the Supreme Being. When he came out of his sweat-house he began to burn tobacco and pray. He began each petition with "Oh, ho, ho, ho," which is a kind of aspiration, and signifies an ardent wish. I observed that all his petitions were only for immediate or present temporal blessings. He began his address by thanksgiving in the following manner:

"O Great Being! I thank thee that I have obtained the use of my legs again; that I am now able to walk about and kill turkeys, etc., without feeling exquisite pain and misery. I know that thou art a hearer and a helper, and therefore I will call upon thee.

"*Oh, ho, ho, ho,*

"Grant that my knees and ankles may be right well, and that I may be able, not only to walk, but to run and to jump logs, as I did last fall.

"*Oh, ho, ho, ho,*

"Grant that on this voyage we may frequently kill bears, as they may be crossing the Scioto and Sandusky.

"*Oh, ho, ho, ho,*

"Grant that we may kill plenty of turkeys along the banks, to stew with our fat bear meat.

"*Oh, ho, ho, ho,*

"Grant that rain may come to raise the Ollentangy about two or three feet, that we may cross in safety down to Scioto, without danger of our canoe being wrecked on the rocks. And now, O Great Being, thou knowest how matters stand; thou knowest that I am a great lover of tobacco, and though I know not when I may get any more, I now make a present of the last I have unto thee, as a free burnt-offering; therefore I expect thou wilt hear and grant these requests, and I, thy servant, will return thee thanks and love thee for thy gifts."

During the whole of this scene I sat by Tecaughretanego, and as he went through it with the greatest solemnity I was seriously affected with his prayers. I remained duly composed until he came to the burning of the tobacco; and as I knew he was a great lover of it, and saw him cast the last of it into the fire, it excited in me a kind of merriment, and I insensibly smiled. Tecaughretanego observed me laughing, which displeased him, and occasioned him to address me in the following manner.

"*Brother,*—I have somewhat to say to you, and I hope you will not be offended when I tell you of your faults. You know that when you were reading your books in town I would not let the boys or any one disturb you; but now, when I was praying, I saw you laughing. I do not think that you look upon praying as a foolish thing; I believe you pray yourself. But perhaps you may think my mode or manner of praying foolish; if so, you ought in a friendly manner to instruct me, and not make sport of sacred things."

I acknowledged my error, and on this he handed me his pipe to smoke, in token of friendship and reconciliation, though at this time he had nothing to smoke but red-willow bark. I told him something of the method of reconciliation with an offended God, as revealed in my Bible, which I had then in possession. He said that he liked my story better than that of the French priests, but he thought that he was now too old to begin to learn a new religion, therefore he should continue to worship God in the way that he had been taught, and that if salvation or future happiness was to be had in his way of worship, he expected he would obtain it, and if it was inconsistent with the honor of the Great Spirit to accept of him in his own way of worship, he hoped that Owaneeyo would accept of him in the way I had mentioned, or in some other way, though he might now be ignorant of the channel through which favor or mercy might be conveyed. He said that he believed that Owaneeyo would hear and help every one that sincerely waited upon him.

A few days after Tecaughretanego had gone through his ceremonies and finished his prayers, the rain came and raised the creek a sufficient height, so that we passed in safety down to Scioto, and proceeded up to the carrying-place. We proceeded from this place down Sandusky, and in our passage we killed four bears and a number of turkeys. Tecaughretanego appeared now fully persuaded that all this came in answer to his prayers, and who can say with any degree of certainty that it was not so?

When we came to the little lake at the mouth of Sandusky, we called at a Wyandot town that was then there, called Sunyendeand. Here we diverted ourselves several days by catching rock-fish in a small creek, the name of which is also Sunyendeand, which signifies rock-fish. They fished in the night with lights, and struck the fish with gigs or spears. The rock-fish here, when they begin first to run up the creek to spawn, are exceedingly fat, sufficiently so to fry themselves. The first night we scarcely caught fish enough for present use for all that were in the town.

The next morning I met with a prisoner at this place by the name of Thompson, who had been taken from Virginia. He told me, if the Indians would only omit disturbing the fish for one night, he could catch more fish than the whole town could make use of. I told Mr. Thompson that if he was certain he could do this, that I would use my influence with the Indians to let the fish alone for one night. I applied to the chiefs, who agreed to my proposal, and said they were anxious to see what the Great Knife (as they called the Virginian) could do. Mr. Thompson, with the assistance of some other prisoners, set to work, and made a hoop-net of elm-bark; they then cut down a tree across the creek, and stuck in stakes at the lower side of it to prevent the fish from passing up, leaving only a gap at the one side of the creek; here he sat with his net, and when he felt the fish touch the net he drew it up, and frequently would haul out two or three rock-fish that would weigh about five or six pounds each. He continued at this until he had hauled out about a wagon-load, and then left the gap open in order to let them pass up, for they could not go far on account of the shallow water. Before day Mr. Thompson shut it up, to prevent them from passing down, in order to let the Indians have some diversion in killing them in daylight.

When the news of the fish came to town the Indians all collected, and with surprise beheld the large heap of fish, and applauded the ingenuity of the Virginian. When they saw the number of them that were confined in the water above the tree, the young Indians ran back to the town, and in a short time returned with their spears, gigs, bows and arrows, etc., and were the chief part of that day engaged in killing rock-fish, insomuch that we had more than we could use or preserve. As we had no salt, or any way to keep them, they lay upon the banks, and after some time great numbers of turkey-buzzards and eagles collected together and devoured them.

Shortly after this we left Sunyendeand, and in three days arrived at Detroit, where we remained this summer.

Some time in May we heard that General Forbes, with seven thousand men, was preparing to carry on a campaign against Fort Du Quesne, which then stood near where Fort Pitt was afterwards erected. Upon receiving this news, a number of runners were sent off by the French commander at Detroit to urge the different tribes of Indian warriors to repair to Fort Du Quesne.

Some time in July, 1758, the Ottawas, Jibewas, Potowatomies, and Wyandots rendezvoused at Detroit, and marched off to Fort Du Quesne, to prepare for the encounter of General Forbes.

The common report was that they would serve him as they did General Braddock, and obtain much plunder. From this time until fall we had frequent accounts of Forbes's army, by Indian runners that were sent out to watch their motion. They espied them frequently from the mountains even after they left Fort Loudon. Notwithstanding their vigilance, Colonel Grant, with his Highlanders, stole a march upon them, and in the night took possession of a hill about eighty rods from Fort Du Quesne; this hill is on that account called Grant's Hill to this day. The French and Indians knew not that Grant and his men were there, until they beat the drum and played upon the bagpipes just at daylight. They then flew to arms, and the Indians ran up under cover of the banks of the Alleghany and Monongahela for some distance, and then sallied out from the banks of the rivers, and took possession of the hill above Grant; and as he was on the point of it, in sight of the fort, they immediately surrounded him; and as he had his Highlanders in ranks, and in very close order, and the Indians scattered and concealed behind trees, they defeated him with the loss only of a few warriors; most of the Highlanders were killed or taken prisoners.

After this defeat the Indians held a council, but were divided in their opinions. Some said that General Forbes would now turn back, and go home the way that he came, as Dunbar had done when General Braddock was defeated; others supposed he would come on. The French urged the Indians to stay and see the event; but as it was hard for the Indians to be absent from their squaws and children at this season of the year, a great many of them returned home to their hunting. After this the remainder of the Indians, some French regulars, and a number of Canadians, marched off in quest of General Forbes. They met his army near Fort Ligoneer, and attacked them, but were frustrated in their design. They said that Forbes's men were beginning to learn the art of war, and that there were a great number of American riflemen along with the redcoats, who scattered out, took trees, and were good marksmen; therefore they found they could not accomplish their design, and were obliged to retreat. When they returned from the battle to Fort Du Quesne, the Indians concluded that they would go to their hunting. The French endeavored to persuade them to stay and try another battle. The Indians said if it was only the redcoats they had to do with they could soon subdue them, but they could not withstand *Ashalecoa,* or the Great Knife, which was the name they gave the Virginians. They then returned home to their hunting, and the French evacuated the fort, which General Forbes came and took possession of, without further opposition, late in the year 1758, and at this time began to build Fort Pitt.

When Tecaughretanego had heard the particulars of Grant's defeat he said that he could not well account for his contradictory and inconsistent conduct. He said, as the art of war consists in ambushing and surprising our enemies, and in preventing them from ambushing and surprising us, Grant, in the first place, acted like a wise and experienced warrior in artfully approaching in the night without being discovered; but when he came to the place, and the Indians were lying asleep outside of the fort, between him and the Alleghany River, in place of slipping up quietly, and falling upon them with their broadswords, they beat the drums and played upon the bagpipes. He said he could account for this inconsistent conduct in no other way than by supposing that he had made too free with spirituous liquors during the night, and became intoxicated about daylight. But to return.

This year we hunted up Sandusky and down Scioto, and took nearly the same route that we had done the last hunting season. We had considerable success, and returned to Detroit some time in April, 1759.

Shortly after this Tecaughretanego, his son Nunganey, and myself went from Detroit (in an elm-bark canoe) to Caughnewaga, a very ancient Indian town, about nine miles above Montreal, where I remained until about the first of July. I then heard of a French ship at Montreal that had English prisoners on board, in order to carry them over sea and exchange them. I went privately off from the Indians, and got also on board; but as General Wolfe had stopped the river St. Lawrence, we were all sent to prison in Montreal, where I remained four months. Some time in November we were all sent off from this place to Crown Point, and exchanged.

Early in the year 1760 I came home to Conocacheague, and found that my people could never ascertain whether I was killed or taken until my return. They received me with great joy, but were surprised to see me so much like an Indian, both in my gait and gesture.

Upon inquiry, I found that my sweetheart was married a few days before I arrived. My feelings I must leave, on this occasion, for those of my readers to judge who have felt the pangs of disappointed love, as it is impossible now for me to describe the emotion of soul I felt at that time.

In the year 1788 I settled in Bourbon County, Kentucky, seven miles above Paris, and in the same year was elected a member of the convention that sat at Danville to confer about a separation from the State of Virginia; and from that year until the year 1799 I represented Bourbon County either in convention or as a member of the General Assembly, except two years that I was left a few votes behind.

II

The Narrative of
Francesco Giuseppe Bressani, S. J.,
Relating His Captivity Among
the Iroquois, in 1644.

THE ITALIAN Jesuit missionary Father Bressani was born in
Rome, 6 May, 1612. At the age of fourteen he entered the novi-
tiate of the Society of Jesus. Becoming zealous to serve as missionary among the American Indians, he went to Quebec in the
summer of 1642, and the following year he was sent among the
Algonquins at Three Rivers.

In April, 1644, while on his way to the Huron country, where
a mission had been established, he was captured by the
Iroquois, who at that time were an exceedingly fierce and even
cannibal nation, perpetually at war with nearly the whole known
continent. By them he was subjected to tortures, but finally was
made over to an old squaw to take the place of a deceased rela-
tive. From her he was ransomed by the Dutch at Fort Orange
(the modern Albany), and by them he was sent to France, where
he arrived in November, 1644.

Despite his terrible experiences among the savages, and his
maimed condition, the indomitable missionary returned to
Canada the next spring, and labored with the Hurons until their
mission was destroyed by the Iroquois four years later.

In November, 1650, Bressani, in broken health, went back to
his native land. Here he spent many years as a preacher and
home missionary. He died at Florence, 9 September, 1672.

The following account of Father Bressani's sufferings among
the Indians is translated from two of his own letters in his book
Breve Relatione d' alcune Missioni nella Nuova Francia, published at Macerata in 1653. *(Editor.)*

FIRST LETTER,

Dated "From the Iroquois, the 15th of July, 1644."

OUR MOST REVEREND FATHER IN CHRIST:

PAX CHRISTI—I know not whether Your Paternity will recognize the handwriting of a poor cripple, who formerly, when in perfect health, was well known to you. The letter is badly written, and quite soiled, because, among other inconveniences, the writer has but one whole finger on his right hand, and can scarcely prevent the paper's being stained by the blood which flows from his yet unhealed wounds. His ink is arquebuse powder [gunpowder rubbed up with water], and his table the bare earth. He writes to you from the land of the Iroquois, where he is now a captive, and would briefly relate what Divine Providence has at last ordained for him.

I set out from Three Rivers, by order of the Superior, the 27th of last April, in company with six Christian Indians and a young Frenchman, with three canoes, to go to the country of the Hurons.

On the evening of the first day, the Huron who steered our canoe, when firing at an eagle, upset us into Lake St. Pierre. I did not know how to swim, but two Hurons caught me and drew me to the shore, where we spent the night, all drenched. The Hurons took this accident for an ill-omen, and advised me to return to our starting point, which was only eight or ten miles off. "Certainly," they cried, "this voyage will not prove fortunate." As I feared that there might be some superstition in this discourse, I preferred to push on to another French fort [Richelieu], thirty miles higher up, where we might recruit a little. They obeyed me, and we started quite early the next morning, but the snow and bad weather greatly retarded our speed, and compelled us to stop at midday.

On the third day, when twenty-two or twenty-four miles from Three Rivers, and seven or eight from Fort Richelieu, we fell into an ambuscade of twenty-seven Iroquois, who killed one of our Indians, and took the rest and myself prisoners. We might have fled, or killed some Iroquois; but I, for my part, seeing my companions taken, judged it better to remain with them, accepting it as a sign of the will of God. . . .

Those who had captured us made horrible cries, and after profuse thanks to the Sun for having in their hands, among the others, a "Black Robe," as they call the Jesuits, they changed the canoes. Then they took from us everything; that is, provisions for all of ours residing among the Hurons, who were in extreme want, inasmuch as they had for several years received no aid from Europe.

Having commanded us to sing, they led us to a little river hard by, where they divided the booty, and scalped the Huron whom they had killed. The scalp was to be carried in triumph on a pole. They also cut off the feet, hands, and most fleshy parts of the body to eat, as well as the heart.

Then they made us cross the lake to pass the night in a retired but very damp spot. We there began to take our sleep bound and in the open air, as we continued to do during the rest of the voyage. . . .

The following day we embarked on a river, and after some miles they ordered me to throw overboard my papers, which they had left me till then. They superstitiously imagined that these had caused the wreck of our canoe. They were surprised to see me grieve at this loss, who had never shown any regret for all else. We were two days in ascending this river to the rapids [of Chambly], which compelled us to land, and we marched six days in the woods.

The next day, which was Friday, the sixth of May, we met other Iroquois going out to war. They added some blows to the many threats they had made; and having related to us the death of one of their party, killed by a Frenchman, was the cause of their commencing to treat me with greater cruelty than before.

At the moment of our capture the Iroquois were dying of hunger; so that, in two or three days, they consumed all our provisions, and we had no food during the rest of the way but from hunting, fishing, or some wild roots, if any were found. Their want was so great that they picked up on the shore a dead beaver already putrefying. They gave it to me in the evening to wash in the river; but, its stench leading me to believe that they did not want it, I threw it into the water. I was paid for that by a severe penance.

I will not here relate all I had to suffer in that voyage. It is enough to say that we had to carry our loads in the woods where there were no roads, but only stones, shoots, holes, water, and snow, which had not yet everywhere melted. We were bare-footed, and were left fasting sometimes till three or four o'clock in the afternoon, and often during the whole day, exposed to the rain, and drenched with the waters of the torrents and rivers which we had to cross.

When evening was come I was ordered to go for wood, to bring water, and to cook when they had any provisions. When I did not succeed, or misunderstood the orders which I received, blows were not spared; still less when we met other barbarians going to fish or hunt. It was not easy for me to rest at night, because they tied me to a tree, leaving me exposed to the keen night air, which was still quite cold.

We at last arrived at their lake [Champlain]. We had to make other canoes, in which I too had to do my part. After five or six days' sailing we landed, and marched for three more.

The fourth day, which was the fifteenth of May, we arrived about the twentieth hour [3 P.M.], and before having as yet taken any food, at a river where some four hundred barbarians were gathered fishing. Hearing of our approach, they came out to meet us. When about two hundred paces from their cabins, they stripped off all my clothes, and made me march ahead. The young men formed a line on each side, armed with sticks, except the first one, who held a knife in his hand.

When I began my march this one stopped my passage, and, seizing my left hand, cleft it open with his knife between the little finger and the ring finger, with such force and violence that I thought he would lay open my whole hand. The others then began to load me with blows till I reached the stage which they had erected for our torture. Then I had to mount on great pieces of bark, raised about nine palms high so as to give the crowd an opportunity to see and insult us. I was all drenched and covered with blood that streamed from every part of my body, and exposed to a very cold wind that made it congeal immediately on my skin. But I consoled myself, seeing that God granted me the favor of suffering in this world some pain in place of what I was under obligation, on account of my sins, to pay in the other with torments incomparably greater.

The warriors came next, and were received by the people with great ceremony, and regaled with the best of all that their fishing supplied. They bade us sing. Judge whether we could do so, fasting, worn down by marching, broken by their blows, and shivering from head to foot with cold.

Shortly after, a Huron slave brought me a little Indian corn, and a captain, who saw me all trembling with cold, at last, at my entreaty, gave me back the half of an old summer cassock, all in tatters, which served to cover rather than warm me.

We had to sing till the warriors went away, and were then left at the mercy of the youths, who made us come down from the scaffold, where we had been about two hours, to make us dance in their fashion; and, because I did not succeed, nor indeed knew how, they beat me, pricked me, plucked out my hair, my beard, etc.

They kept us five or six days in this place for their pastime, leaving us at the discretion or indiscretion of every one. We were obliged to obey even the children, and that in things unreasonable, and often contradictory. "Sing!" cries one. "Hold your tongue!" says another. If I obeyed the first, the latter tormented me. "Stretch out your hand; I want to burn it." Another burned it because I did not extend it to *him.* They commanded me to take fire between the fingers to put in their pipes, full of tobacco, and then let it fall on the ground purposely four or five times, one after another, to make me burn myself picking it up each time.

These scenes usually took place at night. Towards evening the captains cried in fearful voices around the cabins, "Gather, ye young men; come and caress our prisoners!"

On this they flocked together, and assembled in some large cabin. There the remnant of dress which had been given me was torn off, leaving me naked. Then some goaded me with pointed sticks; some burned me with firebrands or red-hot stones, while others used burning ashes or hot coals. They made me walk around the fire on hot ashes, under which they had stuck sharp sticks in the ground. Some plucked out my hair, others my beard.

Every night, after making me sing, and tormenting me as above, they spent eight or ten minutes in burning one of my nails or a finger. Of the ten that I had I have now but one left whole, and even of that they have torn out the nail with their teeth. One evening they burned a nail; the next day the first joint; the day after, the second. By the sixth time they burned almost six. To the hands they applied fire and iron more than eighteen times; and during this torment I was obliged to sing. They ceased torturing me only at one or two o'clock at night. Then they usually left me tied to the ground in some spot exposed to the rain, with no bed or blanket, but a small skin which did not cover half my body, and often even without any covering; for they had already torn up the piece of a cassock which had been given me. Yet, out of compassion, they left me enough to cover what decency, even among them, requires to be concealed. They kept the rest.

For a whole month I had to undergo these cruelties, and greater still, but we remained only eight days in the first place. I never would have believed that man could endure so hard a life.

One night that they were as usual torturing me, a Huron, taken prisoner with me, seeing one of his companions escape torments by siding against me, suddenly cried out, in the middle of the assembled throng, that I was a person of rank, and a captain among the French. This they heard with great attention; then, raising a loud shout in sign of joy, they resolved to treat me still worse, and the next morning I was condemned to be burnt alive, and to be eaten. They then began to guard me more narrowly. The men and children never left me alone, even in the necessities of nature, but came tormenting me to force me to return to the cabin with all speed, fearing that I might take flight.

We left there the 26th of May, and four days after reached the first village of this nation. In this march on foot, what with rain and other hardships, I suffered more than I had yet done. The barbarian then my keeper was more cruel than the first. I was wounded, weak, ill-fed, half naked, and slept in the open air, bound to a stake or a tree, shivering all night with cold and from the pain caused by my bonds.

At difficult places in the road my weakness called for help, but it was refused; and even when I fell, renewing my wounds, they showered blows on me again, to force me to march; for they believed that I did it purposely to lag behind, and so escape.

One time, among others, I fell into a river, and was like to have drowned. However, I got out, I know not how, and in this plight had to march nearly six miles more till evening, with a very heavy burden on my shoulders. They jeered at me and at my awkwardness in falling into the water, and they did not omit, at night, to burn off one of my nails.

We at last reached the first village of this nation, and here our reception resembled the first, but was still more cruel. Besides blows from their fists, and other blows, which I received in the most sensitive parts of my body, they a second time slit open my left hand, between the middle finger and the fore finger, and the bastinade was such that I fell half dead on the ground. I thought I would lose my right eye forever. As I did not rise, because I was unable to do so, they continued to beat me, especially on the breast and head. I should surely have expired beneath their blows had not a captain caused me to be dragged by main strength upon a stage made, like the former one, of bark. There they soon after cut off the thumb and mangled the fore finger of my left hand. Meanwhile a great rain came, with thunder and lightning, and they went away, leaving us exposed naked to the storm, till some one, I know not who, took pity on us, and in the evening took us into his cabin.

Here we were tormented with more cruelty and impudence than ever, without leaving a moment's rest. They forced me to eat filth, and burned some of my fingers and the rest of my nails. They dislocated my toes, and ran a firebrand through one of them. I know not what they did not do to me another time, when I pretended to faint, so as to seem not to see an indecent action.

After glutting their cruelty here, they sent us into another village, nine or ten miles further. Here they added to the torments of which I have spoken that of hanging me up by my feet, either with cords or with chains, which they had taken from the Dutch. By night I lay stretched on the ground, naked and bound, according to their custom, to several stakes, by the feet, hands, and neck. The torments which I had to suffer in this state, for six or seven nights, were in such places, and of such nature, that it is not lawful to describe them, nor could they be read without blushing. I seldom closed my eyes those nights, which, though the shortest of the year, seemed to me most long. "My God, what will purgatory be?" This thought lightened my pains not a little.

In this way of living I had become so fetid and horrible that every one drove me away like a thing of carrion, and they never came near me save to torment me. Scarcely anyone would feed me, although I had not the use of my hands, as they were extraordinarily swollen and putrid. Thus I was still further tormented by hunger, which led me to eat Indian corn raw, not without concern for my health, and made me find a relish in chewing clay, although I could not easily swallow it.

I was covered with loathsome vermin, and could neither get rid of them nor defend myself from them. In my wounds worms were born; more than four fell out of one finger in one day. . . .

I had an abscess in the right thigh, caused by blows and frequent falls, which hindered me from all repose, and especially as I had only skin and bone, and the earth, for bed. Several times the barbarians had tried, but failed, to open it with sharp stones—not without great pain to me. I was forced to employ as surgeon the renegade Huron who had been taken with us. He, on what was supposed to be the eve of my death, opened it for me with four knife-thrusts, and caused blood and matter to issue from it in so great abundance, and with such stench, that all the barbarians of the cabin were constrained to abandon it.

I desired and was awaiting death, though not without some horror of the fire. Still I was preparing for it as best I could, and was commending myself to the Mother of Mercy, who was, after God, the sole refuge of a poor sinner forsaken by all creatures in a strange land, without a language to make himself understood, without friends to console him, without sacraments to strengthen him, and without any human remedy to sweeten his ills.

The Huron and Algonquin prisoners (these are our barbarians), instead of consoling me, were the first to torment me, in order to please the Iroquois.

I did not see the good Guillaume [Cousture], except afterward, when my life was spared me, and the boy who had been taken in my company was no more with me. They had noticed that I had him say his prayers, and that they did not favor. But they did not let him escape torments, for, although he was no more than twelve or thirteen years old, they tore out five of his nails with their teeth; and, on his arrival in the country, they bound his wrists tightly with thongs, causing him the severest pain—and all before me, to afflict me the more. . . .

My days being thus filled up with sufferings, and my nights being spent without repose, I counted in the month five days more than there were; but, seeing the moon one night, I corrected my error. I was ignorant why the savages so long deferred my death. They told me that it was to fatten me before eating me; though they took no means to do so.

One day, at last, they assembled to despatch me. It was the nineteenth of June, which I deemed the last of my life, and I begged a captain to put me to death, if possible, otherwise than by fire; but another man exhorted him to stand firm in the resolution already taken. The first then told me that I was to die neither by fire nor by any other death. I could not believe it, nor do I know whether he spoke in earnest; yet finally it was as he said, because such was the will of God and of the Virgin Mother. . . .

The barbarians themselves marveled at this result, so contrary was it to their intentions, as the Dutch have written to me. I was therefore given, with all the usual ceremonies, to an old woman, to replace her grandfather, formerly killed by the Hurons, but instead of having me burned, as all desired, and had already resolved, she redeemed me from their hands at the expense of some beads, which the French call "porcelain" [wampum].

I live here in the midst of the shadows of death, hearing nothing spoken of but murder and assassination. They have recently murdered one of their own countrymen in his cabin, as useless and unworthy to live.

I have still something to suffer; my wounds are yet open, and many of the barbarians look upon me with no kindly eye. But we cannot live without crosses, and this is like sugar in comparison with the past.

The Dutch gave me hopes of my ransom, and that of the boy taken prisoner with me. God's will be done in time and in eternity! My hope will be still more confirmed, if you grant me a share in your holy sacrifices and prayers, and those of our fathers and brethren, especially of those who knew me in other days.

SECOND LETTER,

Dated "From New Amsterdam, the 31st of August, 1644."

I have found no one to carry the enclosed, so that you will receive it at the same time as the present one, which will give you the news of my deliverance from the hands of the barbarians, whose captive I was. I am indebted for it to the Dutch, and they obtained it with no great difficulty, for a moderate ransom, on account of the little value which the Indians attached to me, from my unhandiness at everything, and because they believed that I would never get well of my ailments.

I have been twice sold: first to the old woman who was to have me burned, and next to the Dutch, dear enough, that is, for about fifteen or twenty doppias [sixty to eighty dollars in gold].

I chanted my "exodus from Egypt" the nineteenth of August, a day that is in the octave of the Assumption of the Blessed Virgin, who was my deliverer.

I was a prisoner among the Iroquois for four months; but small is that compared to what my sins deserve. I was unable, during my captivity, to render to any of those wretched beings, in return for the evil they did me, the good which was the object of my desires; that is, impart to them a knowledge of the true God. Not knowing the language, I tried to instruct, through a captive interpreter, an old man who was dying; but he was too proud to listen to me, answering that a man of his age and standing should teach, and not be taught. I asked him if he knew whither he would go after death. He answered me: "To the Sunset." Then he began to relate their fables and delusions, which those wretched people, blinded by the Demon, esteem as the most solid truths.

I baptized none but a Huron. They had brought him where I was, to burn him, and those who guarded me told me to go and see him. I did so with reluctance; for they had told me falsely that he was not one of our Indians, and that I could not understand him. I advanced towards the crowd, which opened and let me approach this man, even then all disfigured by the tortures. He was stretched upon the bare ground, with nothing to rest his head upon. Seeing a stone near me, I pushed it with my foot towards his head, to serve him as a pillow. He then looked up at me, and either some wisp of beard that I had left, or some other mark, made him suppose I was a foreigner.

"Is not this man," said he to his keeper, "the European whom you hold captive?"

Being answered "Yes," he again cast towards me a piteous look. "Sit down, my brother, by me," said he; "I would speak with thee."

I sat down, though not without horror, such was the stench that exhaled from his already half-roasted body. Happy to be able to understand him a little, because he spoke Huron, I asked him what he desired, hoping to be able to profit by the occasion to instruct and baptize him. To my great consolation I was anticipated by the answer:

"What do I ask?" he said; "I ask but one thing, baptism. Make haste, for the time is short."

I wished to question him as to the faith, so as not to administer a sacrament with precipitation; but I found him perfectly instructed, having been already received among the catechumens in the Huron country. I therefore baptized him, to his and my own great satisfaction. Though I had done so by a kind of stratagem, using the water which I had brought for him to drink, the Iroquois nevertheless perceived it. The captains were at once informed, and, with angry threats, drove me from the hut, and then began to torture him as before.

The following morning they roasted him alive. Then, because I had baptized him, they brought all his members, one by one, into the cabin where I was. Before my eyes they skinned and ate the feet and hands. The husband of the mistress of the lodge threw at my feet the dead man's head, and left it there a long while, reproaching me with what I had done, alluding to the baptism and prayers which I had offered with him, and saying: "And what indeed have thy enchantments helped him? Have they perhaps delivered him from death?"

III

Narrative of Mrs. Mary Rowlandson Who was Taken Captive by the Wamponoags Under King Philip, in 1676.

Written by Herself.

MARY ROWLANDSON was the wife of the Reverend Joseph Rowlandson, the first minister of Lancaster, Massachusetts. On the tenth of February, 1676, during King Philip's War, the Indians destroyed Lancaster, and took her captive. She was treated with gross cruelty, and was sold by her Narragansett captor to a sagamore named Quannopin. After nearly three months of starving and wretchedness she was ransomed for about eighty dollars which was contributed by some women of Boston.

Her own account of her captivity, originally published in 1682, is here given with the omission of nothing but certain reflections that are not essential to the narrative. *(Editor.)*

O N THE 10th of February, 1676, came the Indians with great numbers[1] upon Lancaster. Their first coming was about sun-rising. Hearing the noise of some guns, we looked out; several houses were burning, and the smoke ascending to heaven.

There were five persons taken in one house. The father and mother, and a sucking child, they knocked on the head; the other two they took and carried away alive. There were two others, who, being out of their garrison upon occasion, were set

---

[1] Fifteen hundred Wamponoags, led by King Philip, and accompanied by the Narragansetts, his allies, and by the Nipmucks and Nashaways.

upon; one was knocked on the head, the other escaped. Another there was, who, running along, was shot and wounded, and fell down; he begged of them his life, promising them money, as they told me, but they would not hearken to him, but knocked him on the head, stripped him naked, and split open his bowels. Another, seeing many of the Indians about his barn, ventured and went out, but was quickly shot down. There were three others belonging to the same garrison who were killed. The Indians getting up on the roof of the barn, had advantage to shoot down upon them over their fortification. Thus these murderous wretches went on burning and destroying all before them.

At length they came and beset our house, and quickly it was the dolefulest day that ever mine eyes saw. The house stood upon the edge of a hill; some of the Indians got behind the hill, others into the barn, and others behind anything that would shelter them; from all which places they shot against the house, so that the bullets seemed to fly like hail, and quickly they wounded one man among us, then another, and then a third.

About two hours, according to my observation in that amazing time, they had been about the house before they prevailed to fire it, which they did with flax and hemp which they brought out of the barn, and there being no defence about the house, only two flankers at two opposite corners, and one of them not finished; they fired it once, and one ventured out and quenched it, but they quickly fired it again, and that took.

Now is the dreadful hour come that I have often heard of in time of the war, as it was the case of others, but now mine eyes see it. Some in our house were fighting for their lives, others wallowing in blood, the house on fire over our heads, and the bloody heathen ready to knock us on the head if we stirred out. Now might we hear mothers and children crying out for themselves and one another, "Lord, what shall we do?" Then I took my children, and one of my sisters (Mrs. Drew), hers to go forth and leave the house, but as soon as we came to the door and appeared, the Indians shot so thick that the bullets rattled against the house as if one had taken a handful of stones and threw them, so that we were forced to give back. We had six stout dogs belonging to our garrison, but none of them would stir, though at another time if an Indian had come to the door, they were ready to fly upon him and tear him down. The Lord hereby would make us the more to acknowledge his hand, and to see that our help is always in him. But out we must go, the fire increasing, and coming along behind us roaring, and the Indians gaping before us with their guns, spears and hatchets, to devour us.

No sooner were we out of the house, but my brother-in-law[2] (being before wounded in defending the house, in or near the throat) fell down dead, whereat the Indians scornfully shouted and hallooed, and were presently upon him, stripping off his clothes. The bullets flying thick, one went through my side, and the same, as would seem, through the bowels and hand of my poor child in my arms. One of my elder sister's children, named William, had then his leg broke, which the Indians perceiving, they knocked him on the head. Thus were we butchered by those merciless heathens, standing amazed, with the blood running down to our heels.

My eldest sister being yet in the house, and seeing those woful sights, the infidels hauling mothers one way and children another, and some wallowing in their blood; and her eldest son telling her that her son William was dead, and myself was wounded, she said, "Lord, let me die with them;" which was no sooner said but she was struck with a bullet, and fell down dead over the threshold. The Indians laid hold of us, pulling me one way and the children another, and said, "Come, go along with us." I told them they would kill me; they answered, if I were willing to go along with them they would not hurt me. . . .

There were twelve killed, some shot, some stabbed with their spears, some knocked down with their hatchets. When we are in prosperity, oh, the little that we think of such dreadful sights, to see our dear friends and relations lie bleeding out their heart's-blood upon the ground. There was one who was chopped in the head with a hatchet, and stripped naked, and yet was crawling up and down.

---

[2] Thomas Rowlandson, brother to the clergyman.

I had often before this said, that if the Indians should come, I should choose rather to be killed by them than taken alive, but when it came to the trial my mind changed; their glittering weapons so daunted my spirit that I chose rather to go along with those (as I may say) ravenous bears, than that moment to end my days. And that I may the better declare what happened to me during that grievous captivity, I shall particularly speak of the several removes we had up and down the wilderness.

THE FIRST REMOVE.—Now away we must go with those barbarous creatures, with our bodies wounded and bleeding, and our hearts no less than our bodies. About a mile we went that night, up on a hill within sight of the town where we intended to lodge. There was hard by a vacant house, deserted by the English before, for fear of the Indians. I asked them whether I might not lodge in the house that night; to which they answered, "What, will you love Englishmen still?" This was the dolefulest night that ever my eyes saw. Oh, the roaring and singing and dancing and yelling of those black creatures in the night, which made the place a lively resemblance of hell! And miserable was the waste that was there made of horses, cattle, sheep, swine, calves, lambs, roasting pigs, and fowls (which they had plundered in the town), some roasting, some lying and burning, and some boiling, to feed our merciless enemies; who were joyful enough, though we were disconsolate.

To add to the dolefulness of the former day, and the dismalness of the present night, my thoughts ran upon my losses and sad, bereaved condition. All was gone, my husband gone (at least separated from me, he being in the Bay;[3] and, to add to my grief, the Indians told me they would kill him as he came homeward); my children gone, my relations and friends gone,[4] our house and home, and all our comforts within door and without—all was gone except my life, and I knew not but the next moment that might go too.

There remained nothing to me but one poor, wounded babe;

---

[3] Boston.

[4] Seventeen of her family were put to death or captured.

and it seemed at present worse than death, that it was in such a pitiful condition, bespeaking compassion, and I had no refreshing for it, nor suitable things to revive it. Little do many think what is the savageness and brutishness of this barbarous enemy, those even that seem to profess more than others among them, when the English have fallen into their hands.

THE SECOND REMOVE.—But now (the next morning) I must turn my back upon the town, and travel with them into the vast and desolate wilderness, I know not whither. It is not my tongue or pen can express the sorrows of my heart, and bitterness of my spirit, that I had at this departure; but God was with me in a wonderful manner, carrying me along and bearing up my spirit, that it did not quite fail. One of the Indians carried my poor wounded babe upon a horse. It went moaning all along, "I shall die, I shall die!" I went on foot after it with sorrow that cannot be expressed. At length I took it off the horse, and carried it in my arms, till my strength failed and I fell down with it. Then they set me upon a horse with my wounded child in my lap, and there being no furniture on the horse's back, as we were going down a steep hill we both fell over the horse's head, at which they, like inhuman creatures, laughed, and rejoiced to see it, though I thought we should there have ended our days, overcome with so many difficulties. . . .

After this it quickly began to snow, and when night came on they stopped. And now down I must sit in the snow, by a little fire, and a few boughs behind me, with my sick child in my lap, and calling much for water, being now, through the wound, fallen into a violent fever; my own wound also growing so stiff that I could scarce sit down or rise up.

THE THIRD REMOVE.—The morning being come, they prepared to go on their way. One of the Indians got upon a horse, and they sat me up behind him, with my poor sick babe in my lap. A very wearisome and tedious day I had of it; what with my own wound, and my child being so exceeding sick, and in a lamentable condition with her wound, it may easily be judged what a poor, feeble condition we were in, there being not the least crumb of refreshing that came within either of our mouths from Wednesday night to Saturday night, except only a little cold water. This day in the afternoon, about an hour by sun, we came to the place where they intended, viz., an Indian town called Wenimesset (New Braintree), northward of Quabaug (Brookfield).

This day there came to me one Robert Pepper, a man belonging to Roxbury, who was taken at Captain Beers's fight, and had been now a considerable time with the Indians, and up with them almost as far as Albany, to see King Philip, as he told me, and was now very lately come into these parts. Hearing, I say, that I was in this Indian town, he obtained leave to come and see me. He told me he himself was wounded in the leg at Captain Beers's fight, and was not able some time to go, but as they carried him, and that he took oak leaves and laid to his wound, and by the blessing of God he was able to travel again. Then took I oak leaves and laid to my side, and with the blessing of God it cured me also.

I sat much alone with my poor wounded child in my lap, which moaned night and day, having nothing to revive the body or cheer the spirits of her; but instead of that, one Indian would come and tell me one hour, "Your master will knock your child on the head," and then a second, and then a third, "Your master will quickly knock your child on the head."

This was the comfort I had from them; miserable comforters were they all. Thus nine days I sat upon my knees, with my babe in my lap, till my flesh was raw again. My child being even ready to depart this sorrowful world, they bid me carry it out to another wigwam, I suppose because they would not be troubled with such spectacles; whither I went with a very heavy heart, and down I sat with the picture of death in my lap. About two hours in the night, my sweet babe, like a lamb, departed this life, on Feb. 18, 1676, it being about six years and five months old.

In the morning when they understood that my child was dead, they sent me home to my master's wigwam. By my master in this writing must be understood Quannopin, who was a sagamore, and married King Philip's wife's sister; not that he first took me, but I was sold to him by a Narragansett Indian, who took me when I first came out of the garrison.

I went to take up my dead child in my arms to carry it with me, but they bid me let it alone. There was no resisting, but go

I must, and leave it. When I had been a while at my master's wigwam, I took the first opportunity I could get to look after my dead child. When I came I asked them what they had done with it. They told me it was on the hill. Then they went and showed me where it was, where I saw the ground was newly digged, and where they told me they had buried it. There I left that child in the wilderness, and must commit it and myself also in this wilderness condition to Him who is above all.

God having taken away this dear child, I went to see my daughter Mary, who was at the same Indian town, at a wigwam not very far off, though we had little liberty or opportunity to see one another. She was about ten years old, and taken from the door at first by a praying Indian,[5] and afterwards sold for a gun. When I came in sight she would fall a-weeping, at which they were provoked, and would not let me come near her, but bid me begone, which was a heart-cutting word to me. I could not sit still in this condition, but kept walking from one place to another; and as I was going along, my heart was even over-whelmed with the thoughts of my condition, and that I should have children, and a nation that I knew not ruled over them. Whereupon I earnestly entreated the Lord that he would con-sider my low estate, and show me a token for good, and if it were his blessed will, some sign and hope of some relief.

And, indeed, quickly the Lord answered in some measure my poor prayer; for as I was going up and down mourning and lamenting my condition, my son (Joseph) came to me and asked me how I did. I had not seen him before since the destruction of the town; and I knew not where he was, till I was informed by himself that he was among a smaller parcel of Indians, whose place was about six miles off. With tears in his eyes he asked me whether his sister Sarah was dead, and told me he had seen his sister Mary, and prayed me that I would not be troubled in refer-ence to himself. The occasion of his coming to see me at this time was this: there was, as I said, about six miles from us, a small plan-tation of Indians, where it seems he had been during his captiv-

---

[5] Convert to Christianity.

ity; and at this time there were some forces of the Indians gathered out of our company, and some also from them, among whom was my son's master, to go to assault and burn Medfield. In this time of his master's absence his dame brought him to see me.

Now the Indians began to talk of removing from this place, some one way and some another. There were now, besides myself, nine English captives in this place, all of them children except one woman. I got an opportunity to go and take my leave of them, they being to go one way and I another. I asked them whether they were earnest with God for deliverance. They told me they did as they were able, and it was some comfort to me that the Lord stirred up children to look to Him. The woman, viz., good-wife Joslin, told me she should never see me again, and that she could not find it in her heart to run away by any means, for we were near thirty miles from any English town, and she with a child two years old; and bad rivers there were to go over, and we were feeble with our poor and coarse entertainment. . . .

THE FOURTH REMOVE.—And now must I part with the little company I had. Here I parted with my daughter Mary, whom I never saw again till I saw her in Dorchester, returned from captivity; and from four little cousins and neighbors, some of which I never saw afterwards; the Lord only knows the end of them. We travelled about a half a day or a little more, and came to a desolate place in the wilderness, where there were no wigwams or inhabitants before. We came about the middle of the afternoon to this place, cold, wet, and snowy, and hungry and weary, and no refreshing for man, but the cold ground to sit on, and our poor Indian cheer.

THE FIFTH REMOVE.—The occasion, as I thought, of their removing at this time was the English army's being near and following them; for they went as if they had gone for their lives for some considerable way. Then they made a stop, and chose out some of their stoutest men, and sent them back to hold the English army in play while the rest escaped; and then, like Jehu, they marched on furiously with their old and young. Some carried their old, decrepit mothers; some carried one, and some another. Four of them carried a great Indian upon a bier; but, going through a thick wood with him, they were hindered, and could make no haste; whereupon they took him upon their backs, and carried him, one at a time, till we came to Baquaug River.

Upon Friday, a little after noon, we came to this river. When all the company was come up and were gathered together I thought to count the number of them, but they were so many, and being somewhat in motion, it was beyond my skill. In this travel, because of my wound, I was somewhat favored in my load. I carried only my knitting-work and two quarts of parched meal. Being very faint, I asked my mistress to give me one spoonful of the meal, but she would not give me a taste. They quickly fell to cutting dry trees to make rafts to carry them over the river, and soon my turn came to go over. By the advantage of some brush which they had laid upon the raft to sit on, I did not wet my foot, while many of themselves, at the other end, were mid-leg deep, which cannot but be acknowledged as a favor of God to my weakened body, it being a very cold time. I was not before acquainted with such kind of doings or dangers. A certain number of us got over the river that night, but it was the night after the Sabbath before all the company was got over. On the Saturday they boiled an old horse's leg which they had got, and so we drank of the broth as soon as they thought it was ready, and when it was almost all gone they filled it up again.

The first week of my being among them I hardly eat anything; the second week I found my stomach grow very faint for want of something, and yet it was very hard to get down their filthy trash; but the third week, though I could think how formerly my stomach would turn against this or that, and I could starve and die before I could eat such things, yet they were pleasant and savory to my taste.

I was at this time knitting a pair of cotton stockings for my mistress, and I had not yet wrought upon the Sabbath day. When the Sabbath came they bid me go to work. I told them it was Sabbath day, and desired them to let me rest, and told them I would do as much more work to-morrow; to which they answered me they would break my face.

And here I cannot but take notice of the strange providence of God in preserving the heathen. They were many hundreds, old and young, some sick, and some lame; many had papooses at their backs; the greatest number at this time with us were squaws, and yet they travelled with all they had, bag and baggage, and they got over this river aforesaid; and on Monday they set their wigwams on fire, and away they went. On that very day came the English army after them to this river, and saw the smoke of their wigwams, and yet this river put a stop to them. God did not give them courage or activity to go over after us. We were not ready for so great a mercy as victory and deliverance; if we had been, God would have found out a way for the English to have passed this river as well as for the Indians, with their squaws and children and all their luggage.

THE SIXTH REMOVE.—On Monday, as I said, they set their wigwams on fire and went away. It was a cold morning, and before us there was a great brook with ice on it. Some waded through it up to the knees and higher, but others went till they came to a beaver-dam, and I among them, where, through the good providence of God, I did not wet my foot. I went along that day mourning and lamenting, leaving farther my own country, and travelling farther into the vast and howling wilderness, and I understood something of Lot's wife's temptation when she looked back. We came that day to a great swamp, by the side of which we took up our lodging that night. When we came to the brow of the hill that looked towards the swamp I thought we had been come to a great Indian town, though there were none but our own company; the Indians were as thick as the trees; it seemed as if there had been a thousand hatchets going at once.

THE SEVENTH REMOVE.—After a restless and hungry night there we had a wearisome time of it the next day. The swamp by which we lay was, as it were, a deep dungeon, and an exceeding high and steep hill before it. Before I got to the top of the hill I thought my heart and legs and all would have broken and failed me. What with faintness and soreness of body, it was a grievous day of travel to me. As we went along, I saw a place where English cattle had been. That was a comfort to me, such as it was. Quickly after that we came to an English path, which so took me that I thought I could there have freely lain down and died.

That day, a little after noon, we came to Squaheag,[6] where the

---

[6] Or Squakeag, now Northfield.

Indians quickly spread themselves over the deserted English fields, gleaning what they could find. Some picked up ears of wheat that were crickled down, some found ears of Indian corn, some found ground-nuts,[7] and others sheaves of wheat that were frozen together in the shock, and went to threshing of them out. Myself got two ears of Indian corn, and, whilst I did but turn my back, one of them was stole from me, which much troubled me.

There came an Indian to them at that time with a basket of horse-liver. I asked him to give me a piece. "What," says he, "can you eat horse-liver?" I told him I would try, if he would give me a piece, which he did; and I laid it on the coals to roast; but, before it was half ready, they got half of it away from me; so that I was forced to take the rest and eat it as it was, with the blood about my mouth, and yet a savory bit it was to me; for to the hungry soul every bitter thing was sweet. A solemn sight methought it was to see whole fields of wheat and Indian corn forsaken and spoiled, and the remainder of them to be food for our merciless enemies. That night we had a mess of wheat for our supper.

THE EIGHTH REMOVE.—On the morrow morning we must go over Connecticut River to meet with King Philip. Two canoes full they had carried over. The next turn myself was to go; but, as my foot was upon the canoe to step in, there was a sudden outcry among them, and I must step back; and instead of going over the river, I must go four or five miles up the river farther northward. Some of the Indians ran one way, and some another. The cause of this route was, as I thought, their espying some English scouts, who were thereabouts. In this travel up the river, about noon the company made a stop and sat down, some to eat and others to rest them. As I sat amongst them, musing on things past, my son Joseph unexpectedly came to me. . . .

We travelled on till night, and in the morning we must go over the river to Philip's crew. When I was in the canoe I could not

---

[7] *Apios tuberosa.* The Pilgrims, during their first winter, lived chiefly on these roots. The tubers vary from the size of a cherry to that of a hen's egg, and grow in strings of perhaps forty together.

but be amazed at the numerous crew of pagans that were on the bank on the other side. When I came ashore they gathered all about me, I sitting alone in the midst. I observed they asked one another questions, and laughed, and rejoiced over their gains and victories.

Then my heart began to fail, and I fell a-weeping; which was the first time, to my remembrance, that I wept before them. There one of them asked me why I wept. I could hardly tell what to say; yet I answered, they would kill me. "No," said he, "none will hurt you." Then came one of them and gave me two spoonfuls of meal to comfort me, and another gave me half a pint of peas, which was worth more than many bushels at another time.

Then I went to see King Philip. He bade me come in and sit down, and asked me whether I would smoke—a usual compliment nowadays among the saints and sinners; but this noway suited me; for though I had formerly used tobacco, yet I had left it ever since I was first taken. It seems to be a bait the devil lays to make men lose their precious time. I remember with shame how, formerly, when I had taken two or three pipes, I was presently ready for another, such a bewitching thing it is; but I thank God He has now given me power over it. Surely there are many who may be better employed than to sit sucking a stinking tobacco pipe.

Now the Indians gathered their forces to go against Northampton. Over night one went about yelling and hooting to give notice of the design. Whereupon they went to boiling of ground-nuts and parching corn—as many as had it—for their provision; and in the morning away they went. During my abode in this place Philip spake to me to make a shirt for his boy, which I did; for which he gave me a shilling. I offered the money to my mistress, but she bid me keep it, and with it I bought a piece of horse-flesh.

Afterwards he asked me to make a cap for his boy, for which he invited me to dinner. I went, and he gave me a pancake about as big as two fingers; it was made of parched wheat, beaten and fried in bear's grease, but I thought I never tasted pleasanter meat in my life. There was a squaw who spake to me to make a shirt for her sannup; for which she gave me a piece of beef.

Another asked me to knit a pair of stockings, for which she gave me a quart of peas. I boiled my peas and beef together, and invited my master and mistress to dinner; but the proud gossip, because I served them both in one dish, would eat nothing, except one bit that he gave her upon the point of his knife.

Hearing that my son was come to this place, I went to see him, and found him lying flat on the ground. I asked him how he could sleep so. He answered me that he was not asleep, but at prayer, and that he lay so that they might not observe what he was doing. I pray God he may remember these things now he is returned in safety.

At this place, the sun now getting higher, what with the beams and heat of the sun and smoke of the wigwams, I thought I should have been blinded. I could scarce discern one wigwam from another. There was one Mary Thurston, of Medfield, who, seeing how it was with me, lent me a hat to wear; but as soon as I was gone the squaw that owned that Mary Thurston came running after me and got it away again. Here was a squaw who gave me a spoonful of meal; I put it in my pocket to keep it safe, yet notwithstanding somebody stole it, but put five Indian corns in the room of it; which corns were the greatest provision I had in my travel for one day.

The Indians, returning from Northampton,[8] brought with them some horses and sheep and other things which they had taken. I desired them that they would carry me to Albany upon one of those horses, and sell me for powder; for so they had sometimes discoursed. I was utterly helpless of getting home on foot, the way that I came. I could hardly bear to think of the many weary steps I had taken to this place.

THE NINTH REMOVE.—But, instead of either going to Albany or homeward, we must go five miles up the river, and then go over it. Here we abode awhile. Here lived a sorry Indian, who spake to me to make him a shirt. When I had done it he would pay me nothing for it. But he, living by the river-side, where I often went to fetch water, I would often be putting him in mind,

---

[8] Northampton was attacked March 14, 1676.

and calling for my pay; at last he told me if I would make another shirt for a papoose not yet born he would give me a knife, which he did when I had done it. I carried the knife in, and my master asked me to give it him, and I was not a little glad that I had anything that they would accept of and be pleased with.

My son being now about a mile from me, I asked liberty to go and see him. They bid me go, and away I went; but quickly lost myself, travelling over hills and through swamps, and could not find the way to him. And I cannot but admire at the wonderful power and goodness of God to me, in that though I was gone from home and met with all sorts of Indians, and those I had no knowledge of, and there being no Christian soul near me, yet not one of them offered the least imaginable miscarriage to me. I turned homeward again, and met with my master, and he showed me the way to my son. When I came to him I found him not well; and withal he had a boil on his side, which much troubled him. We bemoaned one another awhile, as the Lord helped us, and then I returned again. When I was returned I found myself as unsatisfied as I was before.

But I was fain to go look after something to satisfy my hunger; and, going among the wigwams, I went into one, and there found a squaw who showed herself very kind to me, and gave me a piece of bear. I put it into my pocket, and came home, but could not find an opportunity to broil it for fear they should get it from me. And there it lay all the day and night in my pocket. In the morning I went again to the same squaw, who had a kettle of ground-nuts boiling. I asked her to let me boil my piece of bear in the kettle, which she did, and gave me some ground-nuts to eat with it; and I cannot but think how pleasant it was to me. I have sometimes seen bear baked handsomely amongst the English, and some liked it, but the thoughts that it was bear made me tremble. But now that was savory to me that one would think was enough to turn the stomach of a brute creature.

One bitter cold day I could find no room to sit down before the fire. I went out, and could not tell what to do, but I went into another wigwam, where they were also sitting round the fire; but the squaw laid a skin for me, and bid me sit down, and gave me some ground-nuts, and bid me come again, and told me they would buy me if they were able. And yet these were strangers to me that I never knew before.

THE TENTH REMOVE.—That day a small part of the company removed about three quarters of a mile, intending farther the next day. When they came to the place they intended to lodge, and had pitched their wigwams, being hungry, I went again back to the place we were before at to get something to eat; being encouraged by the squaw's kindness, who bid me come again. When I was there, there came an Indian to look after me; who, when he had found me, kicked me all along. I went home and found venison roasting that night, but they would not give me one bit of it. Sometimes I met with favor, and sometimes with nothing but frowns.

THE ELEVENTH REMOVE.—The next day, in the morning, they took their travel, intending a day's journey up the river; I took my load at my back, and quickly we came to wade over a river, and passed over tiresome and wearisome hills. One hill was so steep that I was fain to creep up upon my knees, and to hold by the twigs and bushes to keep myself from falling backwards. My head, also, was so light that I usually reeled as I went.

THE TWELFTH REMOVE.—It was upon a Sabbath-day morning that they prepared for their travel. This morning I asked my master whether he would sell me to my husband; he answered, *nux*; which did much rejoice my spirits. My mistress, before we went, was gone to the burial of a papoose, and returning she found me sitting and reading in my Bible. She snatched it hastily out of my hand and threw it out of doors. I ran out and caught it up, and put it in my pocket, and never let her see it afterwards. Then they packed up their things to be gone, and gave me my load; I complained it was too heavy, whereupon she gave me a slap on the face and bid me be gone. I lifted up my heart to God, hoping that redemption was not far off; and the rather because their insolence grew worse and worse.

But thoughts of my going homeward, for so we bent our course, much cheered my spirit, and made my burden seem light, and almost nothing at all. But, to my amazement and great perplexity, the scale was soon turned; for when we had got a little way, on a sudden my mistress gave out she would go no farther, but turn back again, and said I must go back again with her; and she called her sannup, and would have had him go back also, but he would not, but said he would go on, and come to us again in three days. My spirit was upon this, I confess, very impatient, and almost outrageous. I thought I could as well have died as went back. Down I sat, with my heart as full as it could hold, and yet so hungry that I could not sit neither. But going out to see what I could find, and walking among the trees, I found six acorns and two chestnuts, which were some refreshment to me.

Towards night I gathered me some sticks for my own comfort, that I might not lie cold; but when we came to lie down, they bid me go out and lie somewhere else, for they had company they said come in more than their own. I told them I could not tell where to go; they bid me go look; I told them if I went to another wigwam they would be angry and send me home again. Then one of the company drew his sword and told me he would run me through if I did not go presently. Then was I fain to stoop to this rude fellow, and go out in the night I knew not whither. Mine eyes hath seen that fellow afterwards walking up and down in Boston, under the appearance of a friendly Indian, and several others of the like cut.

I went to one wigwam, and they told me they had no room. Then I went to another, and they said the same. At last, an old Indian bid me come to him, and his squaw gave me some ground-nuts; she gave me also something to lay under my head, and a good fire we had. Through the good providence of God, I had a comfortable lodging that night. In the morning, another Indian bid me come at night and he would give me six ground-nuts, which I did. We were at this place and time about two miles from Connecticut River.

THE THIRTEENTH REMOVE.—Instead of going towards the Bay, which was what I desired, I must go with them five or six miles down the river, into a mighty thicket of brush, where we abode almost a fortnight. Here one asked me to make a shirt for her papoose, for which she gave me a mess of broth which was thickened with meal made of the bark of a tree; and to make it better she had put into it about a handful of peas and a few roasted ground-nuts.

I had not seen my son a pretty while, and here was an Indian of whom I made inquiry after him, and asked him when he saw him. He answered me, that such a time his master roasted him, and that himself did eat a piece of him as big as his two fingers, and that he was very good meat. But the Lord upheld my spirit under this discouragement; and I considered their horrible addictedness to lying, and that there is not one of them that makes the least conscience of speaking the truth.

In this place, one cold night, as I lay by the fire, I removed a stick which kept the heat from me; a squaw moved it down again, at which I looked up, and she threw a handful of ashes in my eyes. I thought I should have been quite blinded and never have seen more; but, lying down, the water ran out of my eyes, and carried the dirt with it, that by the morning I recovered my sight again.

About this time they came yelping from Hadley, having there killed three Englishmen, and brought one captive with them, viz., Thomas Reed. They all gathered about the poor man, asking him many questions. I desired also to go and see him; and when I came, he was crying bitterly, supposing they would quickly kill him. Whereupon I asked one of them whether they intended to kill him; he answered me they would not. He being a little cheered with that, I asked him about the welfare of my husband; he told me he saw him such a time in the Bay, and he was well, but very melancholy. By which I certainly understood, though I suspected it before, that whatsoever the Indians told me respecting him was vanity and lies. Some of them told me he was dead, and they had killed him; some said he was married again, and that the governor wished him to marry, and told him that he should have his choice; and that all persuaded him that I was dead. So like were these barbarous creatures to him who was a liar from the beginning.

As I was sitting once in the wigwam here, Philip's maid came with the child in her arms, and asked me to give her a piece of my apron to make a flap for it. I told her I would not; then my mistress bid me give it, but I still said no. The maid told me if I would not give her a piece, she would tear a piece off it. I told her I would tear her coat then. With that my mistress rises up, and takes up a stick big enough to have killed me, and struck at me with it, but I stepped out, and she struck the stick into the mat of the wigwam. But while she was pulling it out, I ran to the maid, and gave her all my apron, and so that storm went over.

Hearing that my son was come to this place, I went to see him, and told him his father was well, but very melancholy. He told me he was as much grieved for his father as for himself. I wondered at his speech, for I thought I had enough upon my spirit, in reference to myself, to make me mindless of my husband and every one else, they being safe among their friends. He told me also, that a while before, his master, together with other Indians, were going to the French for powder; but by the way the Mohawks met with them, and killed four of their company, which made the rest turn back again. For which I desire that myself and he may ever bless the Lord; for it might have been worse with him had he been sold to the French, than it proved to be in his remaining with the Indians.

I asked his master to let him stay awhile with me, that I might comb his head and look over him, for he was almost overcome with lice. He told me when I had done that he was very hungry, but I had nothing to relieve him, but bid him go into the wigwams as he went along, and see if he could get anything among them; which he did, and, it seems, tarried a little too long, for his master was angry with him, and beat him, and then sold him. Then he came running to tell me he had a new master, and that he had given him some ground-nuts already. Then I went along with him to his new master, who told me he loved him, and he should not want. So his master carried him away, and I never saw him afterwards till I saw him at Piscataqua, in Portsmouth.

That night they bid me go out of the wigwam again; my mistress's papoose was sick, and it died that night; and there was one benefit in it, that there was more room. I went to a wigwam and they bid me come in, and gave me a skin to lie upon, and a mess of venison and ground-nuts, which was a choice dish among them. On the morrow they buried the papoose; and afterwards, both morning and evening, there came a company to mourn and howl with her; though I confess I could not much condole with them.

THE FOURTEENTH REMOVE.—Now must we pack up and be gone from this thicket, bending our course towards the Bay towns; I having nothing to eat by the way this day but a few crumbs of cake that an Indian gave my girl the same day we were taken. She gave it me, and I put it in my pocket. There it lay till it was so mouldy, for want of good baking, that one could not tell what it was made of. It fell all into crumbs, and grew so dry and hard that it was like little flints; and this refreshed me many times when I was ready to faint. It was in my thoughts when I put it to my mouth that, if ever I returned, I would tell the world what a blessing the Lord gave to such mean food.

As we went along, they killed a deer, with a young one in her. They gave me a piece of the fawn, and it was so young and tender that one might eat the bones as well as the flesh, and yet I thought it very good. When night came on we sat down. It rained, but they quickly got up a bark wigwam, where I lay dry that night. I looked out in the morning, and many of them had lain in the rain all night, I knew by their reeking. Thus the Lord dealt mercifully with me many times, and I fared better than many of them.

In the morning they took the blood of the deer, and put it into the paunch, and so boiled it. I could eat nothing of that, though they eat it sweetly. And yet they were so nice in other things, that when I had fetched water, and had put the dish I dipped the water with into the kettle of water which I brought, they would say they would knock me down, for they said it was a sluttish trick.

THE FIFTEENTH REMOVE.—We went on our travel. I having got a handful of ground-nuts for my support that day, they gave me my load, and I went on cheerfully, with the thoughts of going homeward, having my burthen more upon my back than my spirit. We came to Baquaug River again that day, near which we abode a few days. Sometimes one of them would give me a pipe, another a little tobacco, another a little salt, which I would change for victuals. I cannot but think what a wolfish appetite persons have in a starving condition; for many times, when they gave me that which was hot, I was so greedy, that I should burn my mouth, that it would trouble me many hours after, and yet I should quickly do the like again. And after I was thoroughly hungry, I was never again satisfied; for though it sometimes fell out that I had got enough, and did eat till I could eat no more, yet I was as unsatisfied as I was when I began.

THE SIXTEENTH REMOVE.—We began this remove with wading over Baquaug River. The water was up to our knees, and the stream very swift, and so cold that I thought it would have cut me in sunder. I was so weak and feeble that I reeled as I went along, and thought there I must end my days at last, after my bearing and getting through so many difficulties. The Indians stood laughing to see me staggering along, but in my distress the Lord gave me experience of the truth and goodness of that promise, Isa. xliii., 2—"When thou passeth through the waters I will be with thee, and through the rivers, they shall not overflow thee." Then I sat down to put on my stockings and shoes, with the tears running down my eyes, and many sorrowful thoughts in my heart. But I got up to go along with them.

Quickly there came up to us an Indian who informed them that I must go to Wachusett[9] to my master, for there was a letter come from the council to the sagamores about redeeming the captives, and that there would be another in fourteen days, and that I must be there ready. My heart was so heavy before that I could scarce speak or go in the path, and yet now so light that I could run. My strength seemed to come again, and to recruit my feeble knees and aching heart; yet it pleased them to go but one mile that night, and there we staid two days.

In that time came a company of Indians to us, near thirty, all on horseback. My heart skipped within me, thinking they had been Englishmen, at the first sight of them; for they were dressed in English apparel, with hats, white neckcloths, and sashes about their waists, and ribbons upon their shoulders. But when they came near there was a vast difference between the lovely faces of Christians and the foul looks of those heathen, which much damped my spirits again.

THE SEVENTEENTH REMOVE.—A comfortable remove it was to me, because of my hopes. They gave me my pack and along we went cheerfully. But quickly my will proved more than my

---

[9] Princeton. The mountain in this town still retains the name of Wachusett.

strength; having little or no refreshment my strength failed, and my spirits were almost quite gone. At night we came to an Indian town, and the Indians sat down by a wigwam discoursing, but I was almost spent and could scarce speak. I laid down my load and went into the wigwam, and there sat an Indian boiling of horse-feet, they being wont to eat the flesh first, and when the feet were old and dried, and they had nothing else, they would cut off the feet and use them. I asked him to give me a little of his broth, or water they were boiling it in. He took a dish and gave me one spoonful of samp, and bid me take as much of the broth as I would. Then I put some of the hot water to the samp, and drank it up, and my spirits came again.

THE EIGHTEENTH REMOVE.—We took up our packs, and along we went; but a wearisome day I had of it. As we went along I saw an Englishman stripped naked and lying dead upon the ground, but knew not who he was. Then we came to another Indian town where we staid all night. In this town there were four English children captives, and one of them my own sister's. I went to see how she did, and she was well, considering her captive condition. I would have tarried that night with her, but they that owned her would not suffer it. Then I went to another wigwam, where they were boiling corn and beans, which was a lovely sight to see, but I could not get a taste thereof. Then I went home to my mistress's wigwam, and they told me I disgraced my master with begging, and if I did so any more they would knock me on the head. I told them they had as good do that as starve me to death.

THE NINETEENTH REMOVE.—They said when we went out that we must travel to Wachusett this day. But a bitter weary day I had of it, travelling now three days together, without resting any day between. Going along, having indeed my life, but little spirit, Philip, who was in the company, came up, and took me by the hand, and said, "Two weeks more and you shall be mistress again." I asked him if he spoke true. He said, "Yes, and quickly you shall come to your master again;" who had been gone from us three weeks.

My master had three squaws, living sometimes with one and sometimes with another: Onux, this old squaw at whose wigwam I was, and with whom my master had been these three weeks.

Another was Wettimore, with whom I had lived and served all this while. A severe and proud dame she was, bestowing every day in dressing herself near as much time as any of the gentry of the land; powdering her hair and painting her face, going with her necklaces, with jewels in her ears, and bracelets upon her hands. When she had dressed herself, her work was to make girdles of wampum and beads. The third squaw was a younger one, by whom he had two papooses.

By that time I was refreshed by the old squaw, Wettimore's maid came to call me home, at which I fell a-weeping. Then the old squaw told me, to encourage me, that when I wanted victuals I should come to her, and that I should lie in her wigwam. Then I went with the maid, and quickly I came back and lodged there. The squaw laid a mat under me, and a good rug over me; the first time that I had any such kindness showed me. I understood that Wettimore thought that if she should let me go and serve with the old squaw she should be in danger to lose not only my service, but the redemption-pay also. And I was not a little glad to hear this; being by it raised in my hopes that in God's due time there would be an end of this sorrowful hour. Then came an Indian and asked me to knit him three pair of stockings, for which I had a hat and a silk handkerchief. Then another asked me to make her a shift, for which she gave me an apron.

Then came Tom and Peter with the second letter from the council, about the captives. Though they were Indians, I gat them by the hand, and burst out into tears; my heart was so full that I could not speak to them; but recovering myself, I asked them how my husband did, and all my friends and acquaintance. They said they were well, but very melancholy. They brought me two biscuits and a pound of tobacco. The tobacco I soon gave away. When it was all gone one asked me to give him a pipe of tobacco. I told him it was all gone. Then he began to rant and threaten. I told him when my husband came I would give him some. "Hang him, rogue," says he; "I will knock out his brains if he comes here." And then again at the same breath they would say that if there should come an hundred without guns they would do them no hurt; so unstable and like madmen they were. So that, fearing the worst, I durst not send to my husband, though there were some thoughts of his coming to redeem and fetch me, not knowing what might follow; for there was little more trust to them to the master they served.

When the letter was come, the sagamores met to consult about the captives, and called me to them to inquire how much my husband would give to redeem me. When I came I sat down among them, as I was wont to do, as their manner is. Then they bid me stand up, and said they were the general court. They bid me speak what I thought he would give. Now knowing that all we had was destroyed by the Indians, I was in a great strait. I thought if I should speak of but a little, it would be slighted and hinder the matter; if of a great sum, I knew not where it would be procured. Yet at a venture I said twenty pounds, yet desired them to take less; but they would not hear of that, but sent the message to Boston, that for twenty pounds I should be redeemed. It was a praying Indian that wrote their letters for them.

About that time there came an Indian to me, and bid me come to his wigwam at night, and he would give me some pork and ground-nuts, which I did; and as I was eating, another Indian said to me, "He seems to be your good friend, but he killed two Englishmen at Sudbury,[10] and there lie the clothes behind you." I looked behind me, and there I saw bloody clothes, with bullet-holes in them. Yet the Lord suffered not this wretch to do me any hurt; yea, instead of that, he many times refreshed me: five or six times did he and his squaw refresh my feeble carcass. If I went to their wigwam at any time they would always give me something, and yet they were strangers that I never saw before. Another squaw gave me a piece of fresh pork, and a little salt with it, and let me her frying-pan to fry it; and I cannot but remember what a sweet, pleasant, and delightful relish that bit had to me, to this day. So little do we prize common mercies when we have them to the full.

THE TWENTIETH REMOVE.—It was their usual manner to remove when they had done any mischief, lest they should be

---

[10] Sudbury was attacked 21st April.

found out; and so they did at this time. We went about three or four miles, and there they built a great wigwam, big enough to hold an hundred Indians, which they did in preparation to a great day of dancing. They would now say among themselves that the governor would be so angry for his loss at Sudbury that he would send no more about the captives, which made me grieve and tremble.

My sister being not far from this place, and hearing that I was here, desired her master to let her come and see me, and he was willing to it, and would come with her, but she, being ready first, told him she would go before, and was come within a mile or two of the place. Then he overtook her, and began to rant as if he had been mad, and made her go back again in the rain; so that I never saw her till I saw her in Charlestown. But the Lord requited many of their ill doings, for this Indian, her master, was hanged afterwards at Boston.

They began now to come from all quarters, against their merry dancing day. Among some of them came one good-wife Kettle. I told her my heart was so heavy that it was ready to break. "So is mine too," said she, "but yet I hope we shall hear some good news shortly." I could hear how earnestly my sister desired to see me, and I earnestly desired to see her; yet neither of us could get an opportunity. My daughter was now but a mile off, and I had not seen her for nine or ten weeks, as I had not seen my sister since our first taking. I desired them to let me go and see them; yea, I entreated, begged, and persuaded them to let me see my daughter, and yet so hard-hearted were they that they would not suffer it. They made use of their tyrannical power while they had it, but through the Lord's wonderful mercy their time was now but short.

On a Sabbath day, the sun being about an hour high in the afternoon, came Mr. John Hoar (the council permitting him, and his own forward spirit inclining him), together with the two fore-mentioned Indians, Tom and Peter, with the third letter from the council. When they came near I was abroad. They presently called me in, and bid me sit down and not stir. Then they catched up their guns and away they ran as if an enemy had been at hand, and the guns went off apace. I manifested some great trouble, and asked them what was the matter. I told them I thought they had killed the Englishman (for they had in the meantime told me that an Englishman was come). They said no; they shot over his horse, and under, and before his horse, and they pushed him this way and that way, at their pleasure, showing him what they could do. Then they let him come to their wigwams.

I begged of them to let me see the Englishman, but they would not; but there was I fain to sit their pleasure. When they had talked their fill with him, they suffered me to go to him. We asked each other of our welfare, and how my husband did, and all my friends. He told me they were all well, and would be glad to see me. Among other things which my husband sent me, there came a pound of tobacco, which I sold for nine shillings in money; for many of them for want of tobacco smoked hemlock and ground-ivy. It was a great mistake in any who thought I sent for tobacco, for through the favor of God that desire was overcome.

I now asked them whether I should go home with Mr. Hoar. They answered no, one and another of them, and it being late, we lay down with that answer. In the morning Mr. Hoar invited the sagamores to dinner; but when we went to get it ready, we found they had stolen the greatest part of the provisions Mr. Hoar had brought. And we may see the wonderful power of God in that one passage, in that when there was such a number of them together, and so greedy of a little good food, and no English there but Mr. Hoar and myself, that there they did not knock us on the head and take what we had; there being not only some provision, but also trading cloth, a part of the twenty pounds agreed upon. But instead of doing us any mischief, they seemed to be ashamed of the fact, and said it was the *matchit*[11] Indians that did it. Oh, that we could believe that there was nothing too hard for God. God showed His power over the heathen in this, as He did over the hungry lions when Daniel was cast into the den.

Mr. Hoar called them betime to dinner, but they ate but little, they being so busy in dressing themselves and getting ready for their dance, which was carried on by eight of them, four men

---

[11] Wicked.

and four squaws, my master and mistress being two. He was dressed in his Holland shirt, with great stockings, his garters hung round with shillings, and had girdles of wampom upon his head and shoulders. She had a kersey coat, covered with girdles of wampom from the loins upward. Her arms from her elbows to her hands were covered with bracelets; there were handfuls of necklaces about her neck, and several sorts of jewels in her ears. She had fine red stockings, and white shoes, her hair powdered, and her face painted red, that was always before black. And all the dancers were after the same manner.

There were two others singing and knocking on a kettle for their music. They kept hopping up and down one after another, with a kettle of water in the midst, standing warm upon some embers, to drink of when they were dry. They held on till almost night, throwing out their wampom to the standers-by. At night I asked them again if I should go home. They all as one said no, except my husband would come for me. When we were lain down, my master went out of the wigwam, and by and by sent in an Indian called James the printer, who told Mr. Hoar that my master would let me go home tomorrow if he would let me have one pint of liquor. Then Mr. Hoar called his own Indians, Tom and Peter, and bid them all go and see if he would promise it before them three, and if he would he should have it; which he did and had it.

Philip, smelling the business, called me to him, and asked me what I would give him to tell me some good news, and to speak a good word for me, that I might go home to-morrow. I told him I could not tell what to give him, I would anything I had, and asked him what he would have. He said two coats, and twenty shillings in money, half a bushel of seed corn, and some tobacco. I thanked him for his love, but I knew that good news as well as that crafty fox.

On Tuesday morning they called their General Court, as they styled it, to consult and determine whether I should go home or no. And they all seemingly consented that I should go, except Philip, who would not come among them.

At first they were all against it, except my husband would come for me; but afterwards they assented to it, and seeming to rejoice in it; some asking me to send them some bread, others some tobacco, others shaking me by the hand, offering me a hood and scarf to ride in; not one moving hand or tongue against it. Thus hath the Lord answered my poor desires, and the many earnest requests of others put up unto God for me.

In my travels an Indian came to me and told me, if I were willing, he and his squaw would run away, and go home along with me. I told them no, I was not willing to run away, but desired to wait God's time, that I might go home quietly and without fear. And now God hath granted me my desire. Oh, the wonderful power of God that I have seen, and the experiences that I have had! I have been in the midst of those roaring lions and savage bears that feared neither God nor man nor the devil, by night and day, alone and in company, sleeping all sorts together, and yet not one of them ever offered the least abuse of unchastity to me in word or action; though some are ready to say I speak it for my own credit; but I speak it in the presence of God, and to His glory. God's power is as great now as it was to save Daniel in the lions' den or the three children in the fiery furnace. Especially that I should come away in the midst of so many hundreds of enemies, and not a dog move his tongue.

So I took my leave of them, and in coming along my heart melted into tears more than all the while I was with them, and I was almost swallowed up with the thoughts that ever I should go home again. About the sun's going down Mr. Hoar, myself, and the two Indians came to Lancaster; and a solemn sight it was to me. There had I lived many comfortable years among my relations and neighbors, and now not one Christian to be seen, or one house left standing. We went on to a farmhouse that was yet standing, where we lay all night; and a comfortable lodging we had, though nothing but straw to lie on. The Lord preserved us in safety that night, raised us up again in the morning, and carried us along, that before noon we came to Concord. Now was I full of joy, and yet not without sorrow; joy to see such a lovely sight, so many Christians together, and some of them my neighbors.

Being recruited with food and raiment, we went to Boston that day, where I met with my dear husband; but the thoughts of our dear children—one being dead and the other we could not tell where—abated our comfort in each other. I was not before so much hemmed in by the merciless and cruel heathen, but now as much with pitiful, tender-hearted, and compassionate Christians. In that poor and beggarly condition I was received in I was kindly entertained in several houses. . . . The twenty pounds, the price of my redemption, was raised by some Boston gentlewomen, and Mr. Usher, whose bounty and charity I would not forget to make mention of. Then Mr. Thomas Shepard, of Charlestown, received us into his house, where we continued eleven weeks; and a father and mother they were unto us. And many more tender-hearted friends we met with in that place. We were now in the midst of love, yet not without much and frequent heaviness of heart for our poor children and other relations who were still in affliction.

The week following, after my coming in, the governor and council sent to the Indians again, and that not without success; for they brought in my sister and good-wife Kettle. About this time the council had ordered a day of public thanksgiving, though I had still cause of mourning; and being unsettled in our minds, we thought we would ride eastward, to see if we could hear anything concerning our children. As we were riding along between Ipswich and Rowley we met with William Hubbard, who told us our son Joseph and my sister's son were come into Major Waldren's. I asked him how he knew it. He said the major himself told him so. So along we went till we came to Newbury; and their minister being absent, they desired my husband to preach the thanksgiving for them; but he was not willing to stay there that night, but he would go over to Salisbury to hear farther, and come again in the morning, which he did, and preached there that day.

At night, when he had done, one came and told him that his daughter was come into Providence. Here was mercy on both hands. Now we were between them, the one on the east, and the other on the west. Our son being nearest, we went to him first, to Portsmouth, where we met with him, and with the major also, who told us he had done what he could, but could not redeem him under seven pounds, which the good people thereabouts were pleased to pay. On Monday we came to Charlestown, where we heard that the Governor of Rhode Island had sent over for our daughter, to take care of her, being now within his jurisdiction; which should not pass without our acknowledgments. But she being nearer Rehoboth than Rhode Island, Mr. Newman went over and took care of her, and brought her to his own house. And the goodness of God was admirable to us in our low estate, in that he raised up compassionate friends on every side, when we had nothing to recompense any for their love. Our family being now gathered together, the South Church in Boston hired a house for us. Then we removed from Mr. Shepherd's (those cordial friends) and went to Boston, where we continued about three quarters of a year. . . .

IV

Capture and Escape of Mercy Harbison, 1792

ON THE 4th of November, 1791, a force of Americans under General Arthur St. Clair was attacked, near the present Ohio-Indiana boundary line, by about the same number of Indians led by Blue Jacket, Little Turtle, and the white renegade Simon Girty. Their defeat was the most disastrous that ever has been suffered by our arms when engaged against a savage foe on anything like even terms. Out of 86 officers and about 1400 regular and militia soldiers, St. Clair lost 70 officers killed or wounded, and 845 men killed, wounded, or missing. The survivors fled in panic, throwing away their weapons and accoutrements. Such was "St. Clair's defeat."

The utter incompetency of the officers commanding this expedition may be judged from the single fact that a great number of women were allowed to accompany the troops into a wilderness known to be infested with the worst kind of savages. There were about 250 of these women with the "army" on the day of the battle. Of these, 56 were killed on the spot, many being pinned to the earth by stakes driven through their bodies. Few of the others escaped captivity.

After this unprecedented victory, the Indians became more troublesome than ever along the frontier. No settler's home was safe, and many were destroyed in the year of terror that followed. The awful fate of one of those households is told in the following touching narrative of Mercy Harbison, wife of one of the survivors of St. Clair's defeat. How two of her little children were slaughtered before her eyes, how she was dragged through the wilderness with a babe at her breast, how cruelly maltreated, and how she finally escaped, barefooted and carrying her infant through days and nights of almost superhuman exertion, she has

87

left record in a deposition before the magistrates at Pittsburgh and in the statement here reprinted. *(Editor.)*

ON the return of my husband from General St. Clair's defeat, and on his recovery from the wound he received in the battle, he was made a spy, and ordered to the woods on duty, about the 23d of March, 1792. The appointment of spies to watch the movements of the savages was so consonant with the desires and interests of the inhabitants that the frontiers now resumed the appearance of quiet and confidence. Those who had for nearly a year been huddled together in the blockhouses were scattered to their own habitations, and began the cultivation of their farms. The spies saw nothing to alarm them, or to induce them to apprehend danger, until the fatal morning of my captivity. They repeatedly came to our house to receive refreshments and to lodge.

On the 15th of May my husband, with Captain Guthrie and other spies, came home about dark and wanted supper; to procure which I requested one of the spies to accompany me to the spring and spring-house, and William Maxwell complied with my request. While at the spring and spring-house we both distinctly heard a sound like the bleating of a lamb or fawn. This greatly alarmed us and induced us to make a hasty retreat into the house. Whether this was an Indian decoy, or a warning of what I was to pass through, I am unable to determine. But from this time and circumstance I became considerably alarmed, and entreated my husband to remove me to some place more secure from Indian cruelties. But Providence had designed that I should become a victim to their rage, and that mercy should be made manifest in my deliverance.

On the night of the 21st of May two of the spies, Mr. James Davis and Mr. Sutton, came to lodge at our house, and on the morning of the 22d, at daybreak, when the horn blew at the blockhouse, which was within sight of our house and distant about two hundred yards, the two men got up and went out. I was also awake, and saw the door open, and thought, after I was taken prisoner, that the scouts had left it open. I intended to rise immediately, but having a child at the breast, and it being awakened, I lay with it at the breast to get it to sleep again, and accidentally fell asleep myself. The spies have since informed me that they returned to the house again, and found that I was sleeping; that they softly fastened the door and went immediately to the block-house, and those who examined the house after the scene was over say that both doors had the appearance of being broken open.

The first thing I knew from falling asleep was the Indians pulling me out of bed by my feet. I then looked up and saw the house full of Indians, every one having a gun in his left hand and tomahawk in his right. Beholding the danger in which I was, I immediately jumped to the floor on my feet, with the young child in my arms. I then took a petticoat to put on, having on only the one in which I slept; but the Indians took it from me, and as many as I attempted to put on they succeeded in taking from me, so that I had to go just as I had been in bed. While I was struggling with some of the savages for clothing, others of them went and took the children out of another bed, and immediately took the two feather beds to the door and emptied them.

The savages immediately began their work of plunder and devastation. What they were unable to carry with them they destroyed. While they were at their work, I made to the door, and succeeded in getting out with one child in my arms and another by my side; but the other little boy was so much displeased by being so early disturbed in the morning that he would not come to the door.

When I got out I saw Mr. Wolf, one of the soldiers, going to the spring for water, and beheld two or three of the savages attempting to get between him and the block-house; but Mr. Wolf was unconscious of his danger, for the savages had not yet been discovered. I then gave a terrific scream, by which means Mr. Wolf discovered his danger and started to run for the block-house. Seven or eight of the Indians fired at him, but the only injury he received was a bullet in his arm, which broke it. He succeeded in making his escape to the block-house. When I raised the alarm, one of the Indians came up to me with his tomahawk as though about to take my life; a second came and placed his hand before my mouth and told me to hush, when a third came with a lifted tomahawk and attempted to give me a blow; but the first that came raised his tomahawk and averted the blow, and claimed me as his squaw.

The commissary, with his waiter, slept in the storehouse near the blockhouse; and, upon hearing the report of the guns, came to the door to see what was the matter; and, beholding the danger he was in, made his escape to the blockhouse; but not without being discovered by the Indians, several of whom fired at him, and one of the bullets went through his handkerchief, which was tied about his head, and took off some of his hair. The handkerchief, with several bullet-holes in it, he afterwards gave to me.

The waiter, on coming to the door, was met by the Indians, who fired upon him, and he received two bullets through the body and fell dead by the door. The savages then set up one of their tremendous and terrifying yells, and pushed forward and attempted to scalp the man they had killed; but they were prevented from executing their diabolical purpose by the heavy fire which was kept up through the portholes from the blockhouse.

In this scene of horror and alarm I began to meditate an escape, and for that purpose I attempted to direct the attention of the Indians from me and to fix it on the blockhouse, and thought if I could succeed in this I would retreat to a subterranean cave with which I was acquainted, which was in the run near where we were. For this purpose I began to converse with some of those who were near me respecting the strength of the blockhouse, the number of men in it, etc., and being informed that there were forty men there, and that they were excellent marksmen, the savages immediately came to the determination to retreat, and for this purpose they ran to those who were besieging the blockhouse and brought them away.

They then began to flog me with their wiping sticks, and to order me along. Thus what I intended as the means of my escape was the means of accelerating my departure in the hands of the savages. But it was no doubt ordered by a kind Providence for the preservation of the fort and the inhabitants in it; for when the savages gave up the attack and retreated, some of the men in the fort had the last load of ammunition in their guns, and there was no possibility of procuring more, for it was all fastened up in the storehouse, which was inaccessible.

The Indians, when they had flogged me away with them, took my oldest boy, a lad about five years of age, along with them, for he was still at the door by my side. My middle little boy, who was about three years of age, had by this time obtained a situation by the fire in the house, and was crying bitterly to me not to go, and making sore complaints of the depredations of the savages. But these monsters were not willing to let the child remain behind them; they took him by the hand to drag him along with them, but he was so very unwilling to go, and made such a noise by crying, that they took him up by his feet and dashed his brains out against the threshold of the door. They then scalped and stabbed him, and left him for dead. When I witnessed this inhuman butchery of my own child I gave a most indescribable and terrific scream, and felt a dimness come over my eyes, next to blindness, and my senses were nearly gone. The savages then gave me a blow across my head and face and brought me to my sight and recollection again. During the whole of this agonizing scene I kept my infant in my arms.

As soon as the murder was effected they marched me along to the top of the bank, about forty or sixty rods, and there they stopped and divided the plunder which they had taken from our house, and here I counted their number and found them to be thirty-two, two of whom were white men painted as Indians. Several of the Indians could speak English well. I knew several of them well, having seen them going up and down the Alleghany River. I knew two of them to be from the Seneca tribe of Indians, and two of them Munsees; for they had called at the shop to get their guns repaired, and I saw them there.

We went from this place about forty rods, and they then caught my uncle John Currie's horses, and two of them, into whose custody I was put, started with me on the horses towards the mouth of the Kiskiminetas, and the rest of them went off towards Puckety. When they came to the bank that descended towards the Alleghany it was so very steep, and there appeared so much danger in descending it on horseback that I threw myself off the horse, in opposition to the will and command of the savages.

My horse descended without falling, but the one on which the Indian rode who had my little boy, in descending, fell and rolled over repeatedly; and my little boy fell back over the horse, but was not materially injured; he was taken up by one of the Indians, and we got to the bank of the river, where they had secreted some bark canoes under the rocks, opposite the island that lies between the Kiskiminetas and Buffalo. They attempted, in vain, to make the horses take the river, and had to leave the horses behind them, and took us in one of the canoes to the point of the island, and there left the canoe.

Here I beheld another hard scene, for as soon as we landed, my little boy, who was still mourning and lamenting about his little brother, and who complained that he was injured by the fall in descending the bank, *was murdered.* One of the Indians ordered me along, probably that I should not see the horrid deed about to be perpetrated. The other then took his tomahawk from his side, and with this instrument of death killed and scalped him. When I beheld this second scene of inhuman butchery I fell to the ground senseless, with my infant in my arms, it being under and its little hands in the hair of my head. How long I remained in this state of insensibility I know not.

The first thing I remember was my raising my head from the ground and feeling myself exceedingly overcome with sleep. I cast my eyes around and saw the scalp of my dear little boy, fresh bleeding from his head, in the hand of one of the savages, and sank down to the earth again upon my infant child. The first thing I remember, after witnessing this spectacle of woe, was the severe blows I was receiving from the hands of the savages, though at that time I was unconscious of the injury I was sustaining. After a severe castigation, they assisted me in getting up, and supported me when up. The scalp of my little boy was hid from my view, and in order to bring me to my senses again they took me back to the river and led me in knee-deep; this had its intended effect. But, "the tender mercies of the wicked are cruel."

We now proceeded on our journey by crossing the island, and coming to a shallow place where we could wade out, and so arrive at the Indian side of the country. Here they pushed me in the river before them, and had to conduct me through it. The water was up to my breast, but I suspended my child above the water, and, with the assistance of the savages, got safely out. Thence we rapidly proceeded forward, and came to Big Buffalo; here the stream was very rapid and the Indians had again to assist me. When we had crossed this creek, we made a straight course to the Connoquenessing Creek, the very place where

Butler, Pa., now stands; and thence we travelled five or six miles to Little Buffalo, which we crossed.

I now felt weary of my life, and had a full determination to make the savages kill me, thinking that death would be exceedingly welcome when compared to the fatigue, cruelties, and miseries I had the prospect of enduring. To have my purpose effected I stood still, one of the savages being before me, and the other walking behind me, and I took from off my shoulder a large powder-horn they made me carry, in addition to my child, who was one year and four days old. I threw the horn on the ground, closed my eyes, and expected every moment to feel the deadly tomahawk. But to my surprise the Indian took it up, cursed me bitterly, and put it on my shoulder again. I took it off the second time, and threw it on the ground, and again closed my eyes, with the assurance I should meet death; but instead of this, the Indian again took up the horn, and with an indignant, frightful countenance, came and placed it on again. I took it off the third time, and was determined to effect it, and, therefore, threw it as far as I was able from me, over the rocks. The savage immediately went after it, while the one who had claimed me as his squaw, and who had stood and witnessed the transaction, came up to me and said: "Well done; you did right and are a good squaw, and the other is a lazy son-of-a-gun; he may carry it himself."

The savages now changed their position, and the one who claimed me as his squaw went behind. This movement, I believe, was to prevent the other from doing me any injury; and we went on till we struck the Connoquenessing at the Salt Lick, about two miles above Butler, where was an Indian camp, where we arrived a little before dark, having no refreshment during the day. The camp was made of stakes driven into the ground, sloping, and covered with chestnut bark, and appeared sufficiently long for fifty men. The camp appeared to have been occupied for some time; it was very much trodden, and large beaten paths went out from it in different directions.

That night they took me about three hundred yards from the camp, up a run, into a large, dark bottom, where they cut the brush in a thicket and placed a blanket on the ground and permitted me to sit down with my child. They then pinioned my arms back, only with a little liberty, so that it was with difficulty that I managed my child. Here, in this dreary situation, without fire or refreshment, having an infant to take care of, and my arms bound behind me, and having a savage on each side of me who had killed two of my dear children that day, I had to pass the first night of my captivity.

But the trials and tribulations of the day I had passed had so completely exhausted nature that, notwithstanding my unpleasant situation, and my determination to escape, if possible, I insensibly fell asleep, and repeatedly dreamed of my escape and safe arrival in Pittsburgh, and several things relating to the town, of which I knew nothing at the time, but found to be true when I arrived there. The first night passed away and I found no means of escape, for the savages kept watch the whole of the night without any sleep.

In the morning one of them left us to watch the trail we had come, to see if any white people were pursuing us. During the absence of the Indian, the one that claimed and remained with me, and who was the murderer of my last boy, took from his bosom his scalp, and prepared a hoop and stretched the scalp upon it. Those mothers who have not seen the like done to one of the scalps of their own children will be able to form but faint ideas of the feelings which then harrowed up my soul. I meditated revenge! While he was in the very act I attempted to take his tomahawk, which hung by his side and rested on the ground, and had nearly succeeded, and was, as I thought, about to give the fatal blow, when, alas! I was detected.

The savage felt at his tomahawk handle, turned upon me, cursed me and told me I was a Yankee; thus insinuating he understood my intention, and to prevent me from doing so again, faced me. My excuse to him for handling his tomahawk was, that my child wanted to play with the handle of it. The savage who went upon the lookout in the morning came back about twelve o'clock, and had discovered no pursuers. Then the one who had been guarding me went out on the same errand. The savage who was now my guard began to examine me about the white people, the strength of the armies going against the Indians, etc., and boasted largely of their achievements in the preceding fall, at the defeat of General St. Clair.

He then examined the plunder which he had brought from

our house the day before. He found my pocket-book and money among his plunder. There were ten dollars in silver and a half-guinea in gold in the book. During this day they gave me a piece of dried venison, about the bulk of an egg, and a piece about the same size the day we were marching, for my support and that of my child; but, owing to the blows I had received from them on the jaws, I was unable to eat a bit of it. I broke it up and gave it to the child.

The savage on the lookout returned about dark. This evening (Monday, the 23d) they moved me to another station in the same valley, and secured me as they did the preceding night. Thus I found myself the second night between two Indians, without fire and refreshment. During this night I was frequently asleep, notwithstanding my unpleasant situation, and as often dreamed of my arrival in Pittsburgh.

Early on the morning of the 24th a flock of mocking-birds and robins hovered over us as we lay in our uncomfortable bed; and sang and said, at least to my imagination, that I was to get up and go off. As soon as day broke, one of the Indians went off again to watch the trail, as on the preceding day, and he who was left to take care of me appeared to be sleeping. When I perceived this I lay still and began to snore, as though asleep, and he also fell asleep. Then I concluded it was time to escape. I found it impossible to injure him for my child at the breast, as I could not effect anything without putting the child down, and then it would cry and give the alarm; so I contented myself with taking, from a pillow-case of plunder stolen from our house, a short gown, handkerchief, and child's frock, and so made my escape; the sun then being about half an hour high.

I struck the Connoquenessing, and went down stream until about two o'clock in the afternoon, over rocks, precipices, thorns, briers, etc., with my bare feet and legs. I then discovered I was on the wrong course, and waited till the North Star appeared. Marking out the direction for the next day, I collected a bed of leaves, laid down and slept, though my feet, being full of thorns, began to be exceedingly painful, and I had nothing for self or babe to eat. The next morning I started early, nothing material occurring. Towards evening a gentle rain came on, and I began to prepare my leaf bed, setting the child down the

while, who began to cry. Fearful of the consequences, I put him
to the breast and he became quiet. I then listened and distinctly
heard footsteps. The ground over which I had travelled was soft
and my foot traces had been followed.

Greatly alarmed, I looked about for a place of safety, and
providentially discovered a large tree which had fallen, into the
top of which I crept. The darkness greatly assisted me and prevented detection. The savage who followed me had heard the
cry of the child and came to the very spot where it had cried,
and there he halted, put down his gun, and was at this time so
near that I heard the wiping stick strike against his gun distinctly. My getting in under the tree and sheltering myself from
the rain, and pressing my boy to my bosom, got him warm, and,
most providentially, he fell asleep, and lay very still during that
time of extreme danger. All was still and quiet; the savage was
listening to hear again the cry. My own heart was the only thing
I feared, and that beat so loud that I was apprehensive it would
betray me. It is almost impossible to conceive the wonderful
effect my situation produced upon my whole system.

After the savage had stood and listened with nearly the still-
ness of death for two hours, the sound of a bell and a cry like
that of a night owl, signals which were given to him by his companions, induced him to answer, and after he had given a most
horrid yell, which was calculated to harrow up my soul, he
started and went off to join them. After his retreat, I concluded
it unsafe to remain there till morning.

But by this time nature was so nearly exhausted that I found
some difficulty in moving; yet, compelled by necessity, I threw
my coat about my child and placed the end between my teeth,
and with one arm and my teeth I carried him, and with the other
groped my way between the trees and travelled on, as I supposed, a mile or two, and there sat down at the root of a tree till
morning. The night was cold and wet, and thus terminated the
fourth day-and-night's difficulties, trials, and dangers!

The fifth day, wet, exhausted, hungry, and wretched, I started
from my resting-place as soon as I could see my way, and on that
morning struck the head-waters of Pine Creek, which falls into
the Alleghany about four miles above Pittsburgh; though I knew
not then what waters they were; I crossed them, and on the

opposite bank I found a path, and on it two moccason tracks, fresh indented. This alarmed me; but as they were before me, and travelling in the same direction as I was, I concluded I could see them as soon as they could see me, and, therefore, I pressed on in that path for about three miles, when I came to where another branch emptied into the creek, where was a hunter's camp, where the two men, whose tracks I had before discovered and followed, had breakfasted and left the fire burning.

I became more alarmed, and determined to leave the path. I then crossed a ridge towards Squaw Run, and came upon a trail. Here I stopped and meditated what to do; and while I was thus musing I saw three deer coming towards me at full speed; they turned to look at their pursuers; I looked too, with all attention, and saw the flash and heard the report of a gun. I saw some dogs start after them, and began to look about for shelter, and immediately made for a large log to hide myself. Providentially I did not go clear to the log; for as I put my hand to the ground, to raise myself so that I might see who and where the hunters were, I saw a large heap of rattlesnakes, the top one being very large, and coiled up very near my face, and quite ready to bite me.

I again left my course, bearing to the left, and came upon the head-waters of Squaw Run, and kept down the run the remainder of that day. It rained, and I was in a very deplorable situation; so cold and shivering were my limbs, that frequently, in opposition to all my struggles, I gave an involuntary groan. I suffered intensely from hunger, though my jaws were so far recovered that, wherever I could, I procured grape-vines, and chewed them for a little sustenance. In the evening I came within one mile of the Alleghany River, though I was ignorant of it at the time; and there, at the root of a tree, through a most tremendous rain, I took up my fifth night's lodgings. In order to shelter my infant as much as possible, I placed him in my lap, and then leaned my head against the tree, and thus let the rain fall upon me.

On the sixth (that was the Sabbath) morning from my captivity, I found myself unable, for a very considerable time, to raise myself from the ground; and when I had once more, by hard struggling, got myself upon my feet and started, nature was so nearly exhausted and my spirits were so completely depressed that my progress was amazingly slow and discouraging. In this almost helpless condition I had not gone far before I came to a path where there had been cattle travelling; I took it, under the impression that it would lead me to the abode of some white people, and in about a mile I came to an uninhabited cabin, and though I was in a river bottom, yet I knew not where I was nor yet on what river bank I had come.

Here I was seized with feelings of despair, went to the threshold of the cabin and concluded that I would enter and lie down and die, since death would have been an angel of mercy to me in such a miserable situation. Had it not been for the sufferings which my infant, who would survive me some time, must endure, I would have carried my determination into execution. Here I heard the sound of a cow-bell, which imparted a gleam of hope to my desponding mind. I followed the sound till I came opposite the fort at the Six Mile Island, where I saw three men on the opposite bank of the river.

My feelings then can be better imagined than described. I called to them, but they seemed unwilling to risk the danger of coming after me, and asked who I was. I told them, and they requested me to walk up the bank awhile that they might see if Indians were making a decoy of me; but I replied my feet were so sore I could not walk. Then one of them, James Closier, got into a canoe to fetch me over, while the other two stood with cocked rifles ready to fire on the Indians, provided they were using me as a decoy. When Mr. Closier came near and saw my haggard and dejected appearance, he exclaimed, "Who in the name of God are you?" This man was one of my nearest neighbors, yet in six days I was so much altered that he did not know me, either by my voice or countenance.

When I landed on the inhabited side of the river the people from the fort came running out to see me. They took the child from me, and now that I felt safe from all danger, I found myself unable to move or to assist myself in any degree, whereupon the people took me and carried me out of the boat to the house of Mr. Cortus.

Now that I felt secure from the cruelties of the barbarians, for the first time since my captivity, my feelings returned in all their poignancy and the tears flowed freely, imparting a happiness beyond what I ever experienced. When I was taken into the house the heat of the fire and the smell of victuals, of both of which I had so long been deprived, caused me to faint. Some of the people attempted to restore me and some to put clothes on me, but their kindness would have killed me had it not been for the arrival of Major McCully, who then commanded along the river. When he understood my situation, and saw the provisions they were preparing for me, he was greatly alarmed; ordered me out of the house, away from the heat and smell; prohibited me from taking anything but a very little whey of buttermilk, which he administered with his own hands. Through this judicious management I was mercifully restored to my senses and gradually to health and strength.

Two of the females, Sarah Carter and Mary Ann Crozier, then began to take out the thorns from my feet and legs, which Mr. Felix Negley stood by and counted to the number of one hundred and fifty, though they were not all extracted at that time, for the next evening, at Pittsburgh, there were many more taken out. The flesh was mangled dreadfully, and the skin and flesh were hanging in pieces on my feet and legs. The wounds were not healed for a considerable time. Some of the thorns went through my feet and came out at the top. For two weeks I was unable to put my feet to the ground to walk. The next morning a young man employed by the magistrates of Pittsburgh came for me to go immediately to town to give in my deposition, that it might be published to the American people. Some of the men carried me into a canoe, and when I arrived I gave my deposition. As the intelligence spread, Pittsburgh, and the country for twenty miles around, was all in a state of commotion. The same evening my husband came to see me, and soon after I was taken back to Coe's Station. In the evening I gave an account of the murder of my boy on the island, and the next morning a scout went out and found the body and buried it, nine days after the murder.

A CATALOG OF SELECTED
DOVER BOOKS
IN ALL FIELDS OF INTEREST

A CATALOG OF SELECTED DOVER BOOKS IN ALL FIELDS OF INTEREST

100 BEST-LOVED POEMS, Edited by Philip Smith. "The Passionate Shepherd to His Love," "Shall I compare thee to a summer's day?" "Death, be not proud," "The Raven," "The Road Not Taken," plus works by Blake, Wordsworth, Byron, Shelley, Keats, many others. 96pp. 5³⁄₁₆ x 8¼. 0-486-28553-7

100 SMALL HOUSES OF THE THIRTIES, Brown-Blodgett Company. Exterior photographs and floor plans for 100 charming structures. Illustrations of models accompanied by descriptions of interiors, color schemes, closet space, and other amenities. 200 illustrations. 112pp. 8⅜ x 11. 0-486-44131-8

1000 TURN-OF-THE-CENTURY HOUSES: With Illustrations and Floor Plans, Herbert C. Chivers. Reproduced from a rare edition, this showcase of homes ranges from cottages and bungalows to sprawling mansions. Each house is meticulously illustrated and accompanied by complete floor plans. 256pp. 9⅜ x 12¼.

0-486-45596-3

101 GREAT AMERICAN POEMS, Edited by The American Poetry & Literacy Project. Rich treasury of verse from the 19th and 20th centuries includes works by Edgar Allan Poe, Robert Frost, Walt Whitman, Langston Hughes, Emily Dickinson, T. S. Eliot, other notables. 96pp. 5³⁄₁₆ x 8¼. 0-486-40158-8

101 GREAT SAMURAI PRINTS, Utagawa Kuniyoshi. Kuniyoshi was a master of the warrior woodblock print — and these 18th-century illustrations represent the pinnacle of his craft. Full-color portraits of renowned Japanese samurais pulse with movement, passion, and remarkably fine detail. 112pp. 8⅜ x 11. 0-486-46523-3

ABC OF BALLET, Janet Grosser. Clearly worded, abundantly illustrated little guide defines basic ballet-related terms: arabesque, battement, pas de chat, relevé, sissonne, many others. Pronunciation guide included. Excellent primer. 48pp. 4³⁄₁₆ x 5¾.

0-486-40871-X

ACCESSORIES OF DRESS: An Illustrated Encyclopedia, Katherine Lester and Bess Viola Oerke. Illustrations of hats, veils, wigs, cravats, shawls, shoes, gloves, and other accessories enhance an engaging commentary that reveals the humor and charm of the many-sided story of accessorized apparel. 644 figures and 59 plates. 608pp. 6⅛ x 9¼.

0-486-43378-1

ADVENTURES OF HUCKLEBERRY FINN, Mark Twain. Join Huck and Jim as their boyhood adventures along the Mississippi River lead them into a world of excitement, danger, and self-discovery. Humorous narrative, lyrical descriptions of the Mississippi valley, and memorable characters. 224pp. 5³⁄₁₆ x 8¼. 0-486-28061-6

ALICE STARMORE'S BOOK OF FAIR ISLE KNITTING, Alice Starmore. A noted designer from the region of Scotland's Fair Isle explores the history and techniques of this distinctive, stranded-color knitting style and provides copious illustrated instructions for 14 original knitwear designs. 208pp. 8⅜ x 10⅞. 0-486-47218-3

Browse over 9,000 books at www.doverpublications.com

ALICE'S ADVENTURES IN WONDERLAND, Lewis Carroll. Beloved classic about a little girl lost in a topsy-turvy land and her encounters with the White Rabbit, March Hare, Mad Hatter, Cheshire Cat, and other delightfully improbable characters. 42 illustrations by Sir John Tenniel. 96pp. 5³⁄₁₆ x 8¼.   0-486-27543-4

AMERICA'S LIGHTHOUSES: An Illustrated History, Francis Ross Holland. Profusely illustrated fact-filled survey of American lighthouses since 1716. Over 200 stations — East, Gulf, and West coasts, Great Lakes, Hawaii, Alaska, Puerto Rico, the Virgin Islands, and the Mississippi and St. Lawrence Rivers. 240pp. 8 x 10¾.
0-486-25576-X

AN ENCYCLOPEDIA OF THE VIOLIN, Alberto Bachmann. Translated by Frederick H. Martens. Introduction by Eugene Ysaye. First published in 1925, this renowned reference remains unsurpassed as a source of essential information, from construction and evolution to repertoire and technique. Includes a glossary and 73 illustrations. 496pp. 6⅛ x 9¼.   0-486-46618-3

ANIMALS: 1,419 Copyright-Free Illustrations of Mammals, Birds, Fish, Insects, etc., Selected by Jim Harter. Selected for its visual impact and ease of use, this outstanding collection of wood engravings presents over 1,000 species of animals in extremely lifelike poses. Includes mammals, birds, reptiles, amphibians, fish, insects, and other invertebrates. 284pp. 9 x 12.   0-486-23766-4

THE ANNALS, Tacitus. Translated by Alfred John Church and William Jackson Brodribb. This vital chronicle of Imperial Rome, written by the era's great historian, spans A.D. 14-68 and paints incisive psychological portraits of major figures, from Tiberius to Nero. 416pp. 5³⁄₁₆ x 8¼.   0-486-45236-0

ANTIGONE, Sophocles. Filled with passionate speeches and sensitive probing of moral and philosophical issues, this powerful and often-performed Greek drama reveals the grim fate that befalls the children of Oedipus. Footnotes. 64pp. 5³⁄₁₆ x 8 ¼.   0-486-27804-2

ART DECO DECORATIVE PATTERNS IN FULL COLOR, Christian Stoll. Reprinted from a rare 1910 portfolio, 160 sensuous and exotic images depict a breathtaking array of florals, geometrics, and abstracts — all elegant in their stark simplicity. 64pp. 8⅜ x 11.   0-486-44862-2

THE ARTHUR RACKHAM TREASURY: 86 Full-Color Illustrations, Arthur Rackham. Selected and Edited by Jeff A. Menges. A stunning treasury of 86 full-page plates span the famed English artist's career, from *Rip Van Winkle* (1905) to masterworks such as *Undine, A Midsummer Night's Dream,* and *Wind in the Willows* (1939). 96pp. 8⅜ x 11.
0-486-44685-9

THE AUTHENTIC GILBERT & SULLIVAN SONGBOOK, W. S. Gilbert and A. S. Sullivan. The most comprehensive collection available, this songbook includes selections from every one of Gilbert and Sullivan's light operas. Ninety-two numbers are presented uncut and unedited, and in their original keys. 410pp. 9 x 12.
0-486-23482-7

THE AWAKENING, Kate Chopin. First published in 1899, this controversial novel of a New Orleans wife's search for love outside a stifling marriage shocked readers. Today, it remains a first-rate narrative with superb characterization. New introductory Note. 128pp. 5³⁄₁₆ x 8¼.   0-486-27786-0

BASIC DRAWING, Louis Priscilla. Beginning with perspective, this commonsense manual progresses to the figure in movement, light and shade, anatomy, drapery, composition, trees and landscape, and outdoor sketching. Black-and-white illustrations throughout. 128pp. 8⅜ x 11.   0-486-45815-6

Browse over 9,000 books at www.doverpublications.com